STAMPED METAL JEWELRY

Creative techniques & designs for making custom jewelry

LISA NIVEN KELLY
CREATOR OF BEADUCATION

EDITOR Elaine Lipson
ART DIRECTOR Liz Quan
COVER AND INTERIOR DESIGN Nice Kern LLC
PROJECT PHOTOGRAPHY Brad Bartholomew
PHOTO STYLIST Pamela Chavez
PROCESS PHOTOGRAPHY Melinda Prabhu
PRODUCTION Katherine Jackson

Interweave Press LLC
201 East Fourth Street
Loveland, CO 80537-5655 USA
interweavestore.com

Printed in China by Imago.

Library of Congress Cataloging-in-Publication Data

Kelly, Lisa Niven.
Stamped metal jewelry:
creative techniques and designs for making custom jewelry / Lisa Niven Kelly.
p. cm.
Includes index.
ISBN 978-1-59668-177-4 (pbk.)
1. Jewelry making. 2. Metal-work. I. Title.
TT212.K397 2010
739.27--dc22
2009043010

10 9 8 7 6 5 4 3 2 1

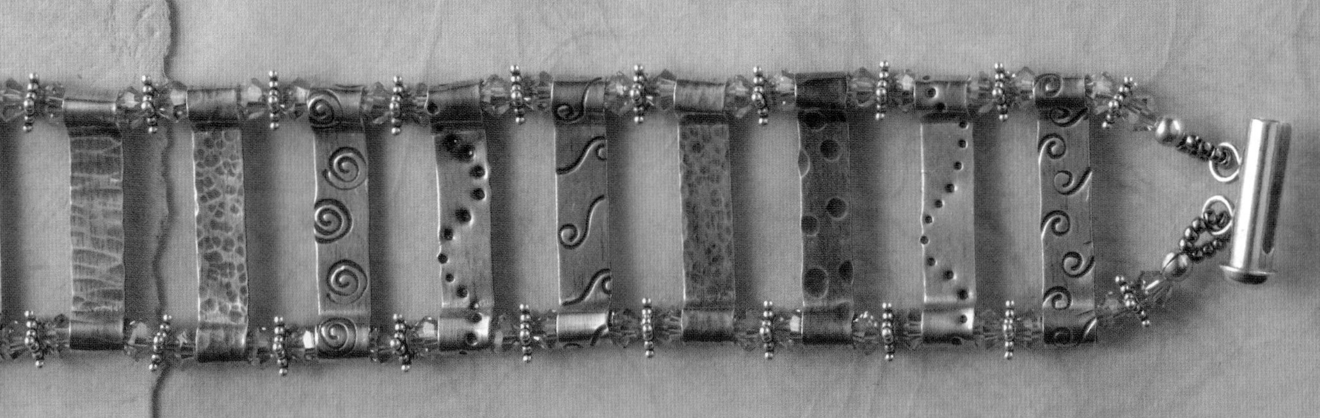

ACKNOWLEDGMENTS

Putting this book together has been an amazing adventure. As with anything, it takes a village, and there are a lot of folks to thank in my little town. A big huge thanks to the folks at Interweave and my editor, Elaine Lipson, for your encouragement and endless patience. To my contributing artists, Tracy Stanley, Lisa Claxton, Kriss Silva, Kate Richbourg, Connie Fox, and Janice Berkebile, thank you for lending your mad skills to my book. I could not have even attempted this book without the overwhelming support of my team at Beaducation. Y'all are the best. Thanks to Mary Carroll for all her proofreading help. To my abundantly talented friends Barb Switzer and Kate Richbourg, thanks for your technical and writing help and incredible support. Thanks to my photographer, Mindy Prabhu; you are so talented, and thank you for sharing that with me. Barb, Kate, and Mindy, this book would not have happened without you.

To my friends and family who pulled me through this last year with so much support and love: Jen, John, Nancy, Thea, Jon, Mo, Jack, Marian, Mike, Carol, Dave T., and Daisy: THANK YOU, THANK YOU, THANK YOU. To my husband, "the most supportive man in the world," and my daughters, Izzy and Lucy; thank you for putting up with my late nights at the office.

A big thank you to my biggest fans in the world: my mom, Bonnie; my dad, John; and my stepmom, Yvonne. You have always supported my decision to choose a career in art with constant smiles and encouragement. Finally, I would like to dedicate this book to my stepfather, Frank Henry, the bravest and most loving man I have ever met. I miss you; this book and all its efforts are for you.

CONTENTS

COVER PROJECTS, CLOCKWISE FROM TOP LEFT:
Crisscross Stamped and Riveted Earrings;
Easy Stamped Pendant (variation);
Leather Cuff; Easy Stamped Pendant (variation);
Say It on Your Wrist; Linked Shapes Bracelet

INTRODUCTION

It all started with some letter stamps and metal sheet (oh yeah, and a hammer and bench block!). I loved making my first piece of stamped metal jewelry and have never looked back. That was six years ago, and the piece was a simple cuff bracelet that came to be known as my *Say It on Your Wrist* design. Soon my work space was cluttered with stamps, metal, and odd new tools. I taught and taught, and my students loved stamping as much as I did.

All those years of learning and teaching have come together between the covers of this book. I am so excited to put it all together to share with you. Stamping itself is a fairly basic technique, but my goal for this book is to show how compatible it can be with other basic wirework and metalsmithing techniques. Stamping can add the little extra something that makes your design special and truly personal. I cover a variety of techniques in this book, including riveting, hammering, dapping, and, of course, stamping. My hope is that you will use these techniques as inspiration as you improve your aptitude and skill.

Think of this book as a guidebook, a springboard, or a road map to send you down the path of stamped and riveted jewelry. Read each technique section carefully, and practice, practice, practice. Use the enclosed DVD for live demonstrations of stamping techniques as you go along. Every project in this book is designed to incorporate different skills. When you've mastered these new skills, go ahead and create new designs of your own! Stamp, dap, and rivet away!

Maya Raine
TO THINE OWN SELF BE TRUE
I BELIEVE IN MAGIC

MATERIALS & TOOLS

As you begin to make stamped metal jewelry, you'll get to know and enjoy the properties of different metals—the essential material for this craft—and learn how to get the effects you want from each one. Keep a supply of different prefabricated blanks and pieces of sheet metal for whenever inspiration strikes, or practice time becomes available.

While the list of tools in this chapter may seem extensive, it's okay to start small for simpler projects, or buy tools to share with creative friends. As your skills grow and your ideas multiply, you can build on the basics and expand your creative possibilities.

TOOLS

Using the right tool for the right job is the key to successful stamping and jewelry making. As with anything else, you pay for quality. My advice is to purchase the highest-quality tool that you can afford at the time. This way, you will avoid throwing away and replacing cheaper tools, which might break or wear, becoming unusable.

Stamps

Metal stamps are the core of your stamped metal jewelry tool kit. With the letters of the alphabet and numbers from zero to nine, along with a few design stamps, you can express anything! The best stamp sets are made of tool-hardened steel, which will stand the test of time.

LETTER/NUMBER STAMP SETS Stamp sets of letters and numbers are available in various sizes and fonts. You'll find a wide variety of letter sets in a basic uppercase Gothic font; other fonts are also available, but they may cost a bit more. Look for good-quality sets that are sold in a compartmentalized box containing a slot for each letter. Trust me, when you are stamping out your words, knowing exactly where to find each letter makes designing much easier. Lower-quality stamp sets have letters with edges that are less sharp and will not yield a crisp impression. I also find that cheaper sets have letters that are inconsistent in size.

DESIGN STAMPS Design stamps come in a variety of shapes, motifs, and sizes. These stamps can add a bit of pizzazz to your designs and can be used in repeats or combinations to make simple or complex patterns.

Essentials

These essential items are the foundation of your stamped metal studio; they'll aid you in working with the small pieces of metal that jewelry making requires and give you a good surface for stamping activities. Make sure that you work on a strong table. A weak or wobbly table—such as a card table or a TV tray—absorbs the blow, and again, your impression will not be deep and sharp. And safety glasses are a must!

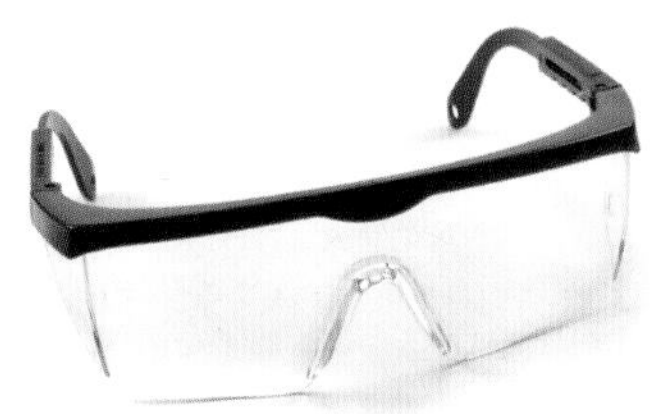

SAFETY GLASSES Wear safety glasses when working with hammers and design stamps, sawing and drilling, punching holes, working with chemical solutions, and performing other metalsmithing activities. It's extremely important to keep your eyes protected.

BENCH BLOCK A steel bench block is the ideal surface for stamping. A hard surface underneath the metal ensures a sharp impression; other surfaces will absorb the blow and cause the impression to be weak. Steel bench blocks can be found in a variety of sizes and shapes; I use a 2½" or 4" (6.5 cm or 10 cm) square block.

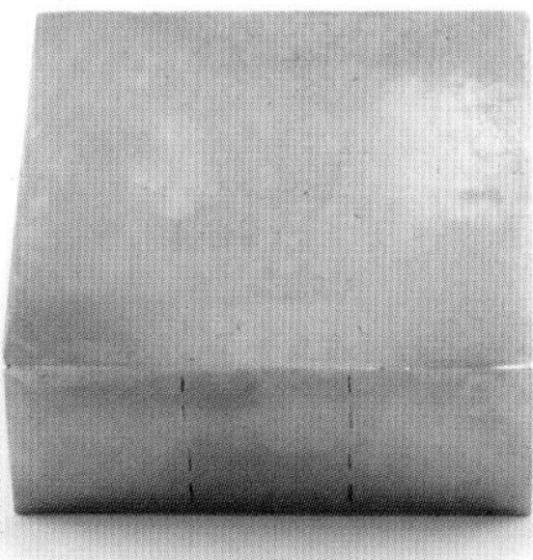

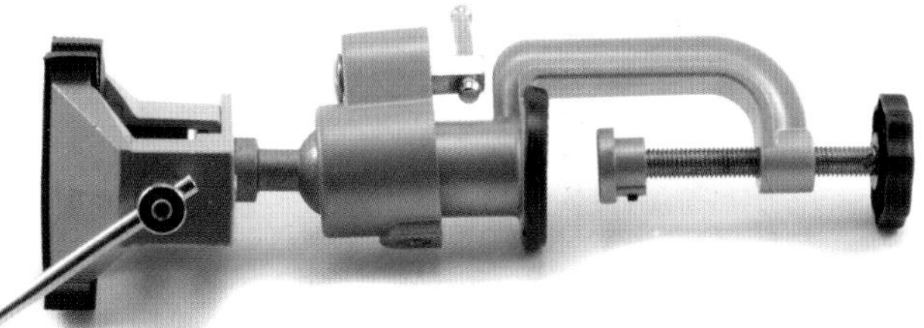

TABLE VISE WITH PLASTIC OR RUBBER CLAMP CAPS The jaws of a table vise can be adjusted to securely clamp an object in place. The vise also has a clamp that secures to the worktable, making it portable. The covers on the inside of the clamps allow you to pinch down on and hold metal without marring or flattening it.

CENTER PUNCH This tool has a tip that comes to a point and is used to make a slight dent in metal before drilling, giving a starting and resting point for the drill bit. You can find a center punch at most hardware stores.

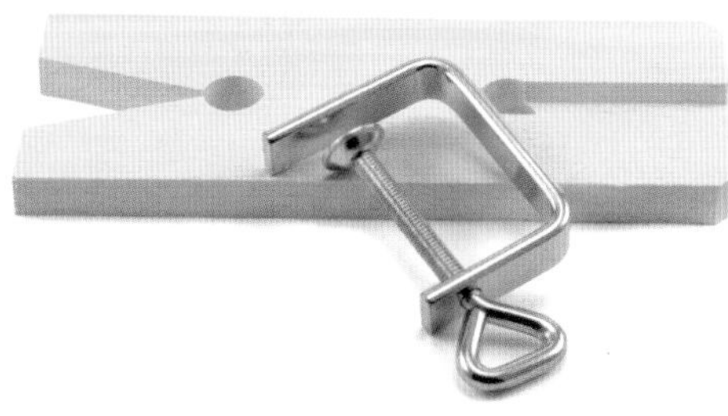

BENCH PIN A bench pin is a wooden V-slot piece of wood that clamps to your table or bench. This provides the perfect stabilizing surface for sawing or filing metal.

RING CLAMP This wooden clamp can be held in the hand or stabilized against a bench pin to hold rings or smaller metal pieces when a tight grip is needed.

Hammers

Even if you haven't spent much time wielding hammers, you'll get plenty of practice with these versatile tools as you make stamped metal jewelry. Your hammers will become your best friends as they help you stamp out beautiful designs.

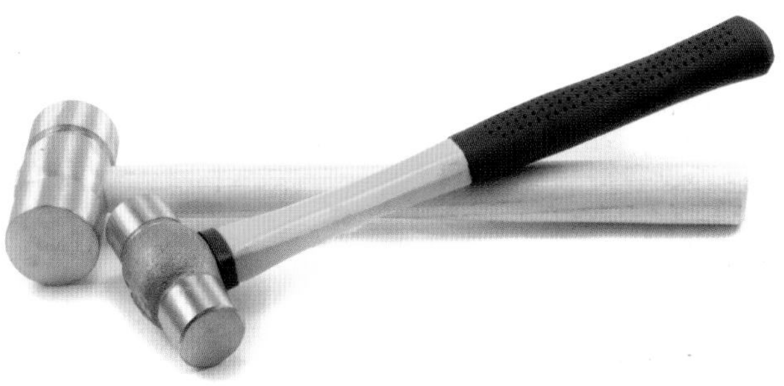

STAMPING HAMMER Your stamping hammer should weigh at least 1 pound, and preferably have a brass head. Do not use a jewelry hammer because the stamps will mar the head and ruin the hammer. Design stamps have more detail than letter stamps do and are harder to stamp evenly; if you find yourself struggling with design stamps, bump your hammer up to 2 or 3 pounds.

CHASING HAMMER A chasing hammer has a flat, slightly rounded head on one side and a ball head on the other. It is used to flatten and shape metal.

TEXTURE HAMMER Texture hammers have designs ground into the heads. The design is transferred onto metal by striking it with the head of the hammer.

RIVETING HAMMER This tool has a small, flat, rounded, or square head on one side and a tapered thin head on the other. The tapered head is used to "mushroom" the head of a wire rivet, and the flat end is used to tap the rivet to secure.

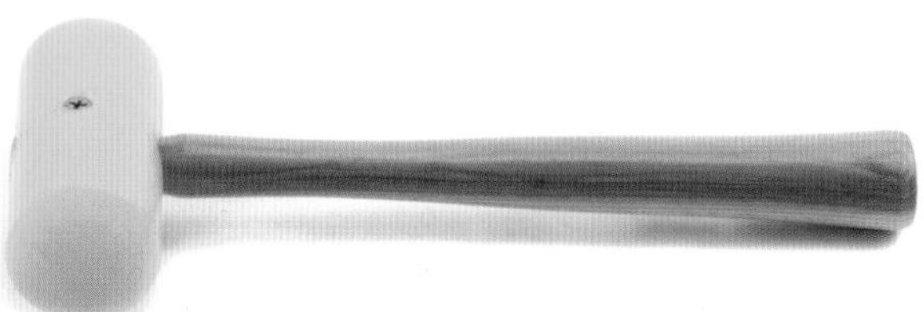

PLASTIC MALLET This hammer is used to shape metal sheet or wire without marking or thinning out the gauge.

Pliers

Pliers help you bend and shape metal and wire, and each kind has its own advantages. Using the right pair of pliers at each step in the jewelry-making process will help you get professional results.

CHAIN-NOSE PLIERS Chain-nose pliers have flat inside jaws and are used to hold and manipulate wire.

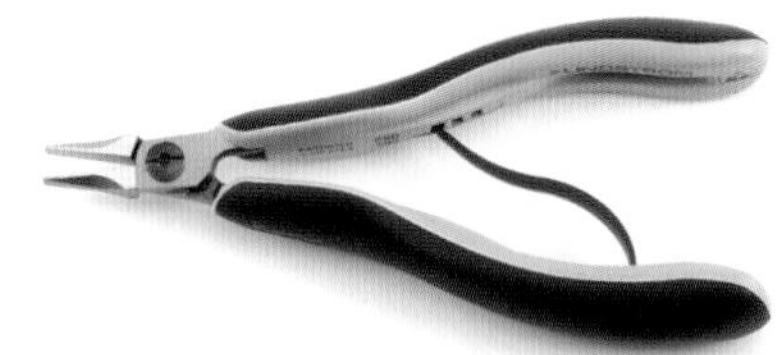

FLAT-NOSE PLIERS Flat-nose pliers are useful as a second hand when opening and closing jump rings.

ROUND-NOSE PLIERS Round-nose pliers are used to make loops and circles.

LARGE WRAP 'N' TAP PLIERS This tool has a triple-barrel stepped round nose. The steps on this plier measure 13 mm, 16 mm, and 20 mm. Use your wrap-and-tap pliers to shape rings or make large loops.

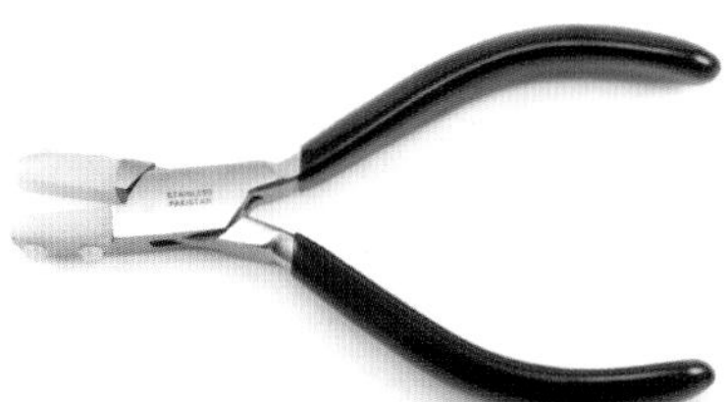

NYLON-JAW PLIERS The jaws on these pliers are made from nylon, allowing manipulation of the wire without marring. Nylon-jaw pliers can also be used to straighten wire.

STEPPED ROUND-NOSE PLIERS Stepped round-nose pliers (sometimes called coiling pliers) have one flat jaw and one stepped round jaw. These pliers are especially helpful in making evenly sized loops.

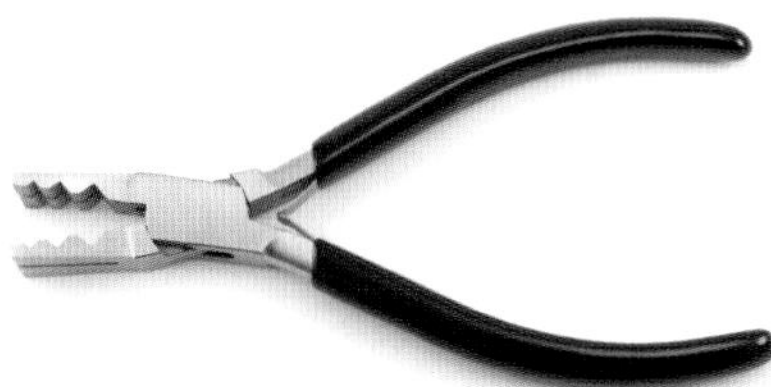

TUBE-CUTTING PLIERS Tube-cutting pliers hold metal tube; a narrow groove down the center of the jaws guides the saw blade when cutting the tube.

Cutting, Punching, and Filing Tools

Design possibilities increase with your skills in cutting your own shapes from metal, punching or drilling holes accurately and neatly, and filing edges for smoothness and shape. These tools make these shaping activities easy, fun, and safe.

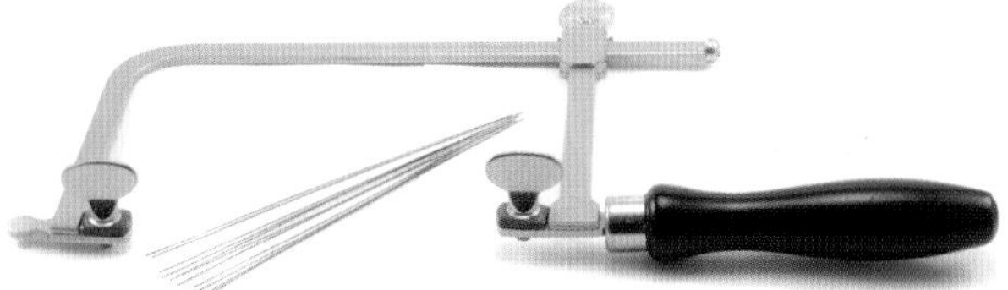

JEWELER'S SAW, SAW BLADES, AND CUT LUBE Use a jeweler's saw with saw blades to cut sheet metal or tubing. Saw blades come in a variety of sizes. In this book, we use 4/0 (pronounced "4, ought") and 2/0. I use cut lube lubricant on blades to make cutting easier and more precise.

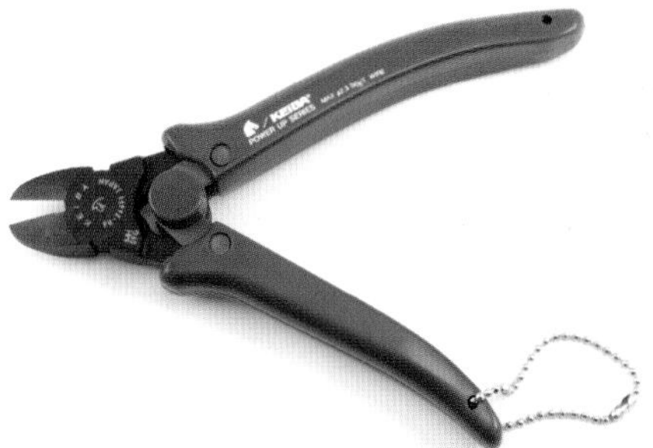

HEAVY-DUTY CUTTERS Choose a heavy-duty cutter capable of cutting metal up to 12-gauge or 1.5 mm thick. With a heavy cutter like this, it is best to cut at the back of the blades (closest to the joint, not the tip).

FLUSH CUTTERS These are wire nippers that cut wire flush, leaving very little "pinch" on the end of the wire.

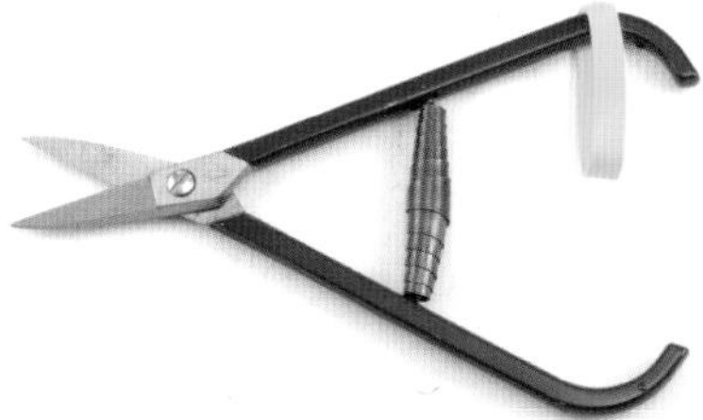

METAL SHEARS This tool cuts sheet metal with a scissors-like action.

DISC CUTTER A disc cutter is a metal block with various sizes of circle punches, used to cut circular shapes. To cut, line up sheet metal with the appropriate hole in the cutter, insert the corresponding punch, and strike hard a few times with a brass-head mallet. It is important to use a quality disc cutter; a cheap one will do a substandard job and is a waste of money.

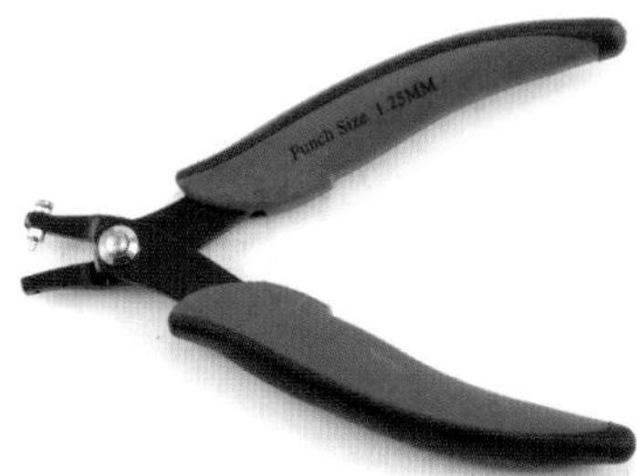

HOLE-PUNCH PLIERS These are pliers with a pin (punch) on one side and a corresponding hole in the jaw on the other. These often come with removable and replaceable pins. A leather hole-punch pliers is typically not strong enough to punch through metal.

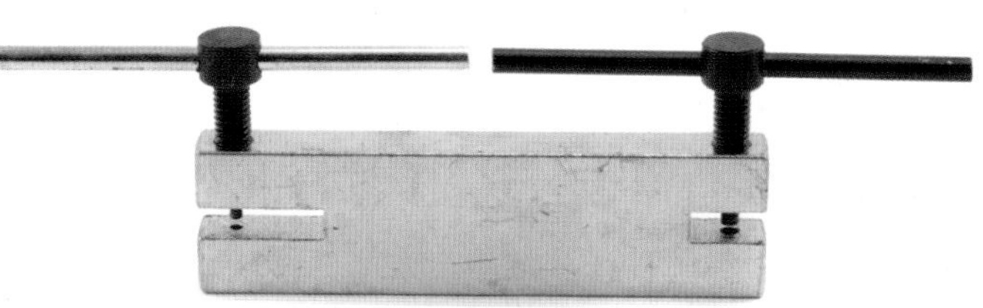

SCREW-DOWN HOLE PUNCH This tool punches two different-size holes. The silver-topped side makes a 1.6 mm (close to a 14-gauge) hole, and the black-topped side makes a 2.3 mm (close to an 11-gauge) hole.

DRILL AND DRILL BITS The most common drill for jewelry work is a flexible shaft drill or a Dremel tool. Drill bits are available in a variety of sizes. Consult the chart on page 25 to determine the correct drill bit for a specific hole size.

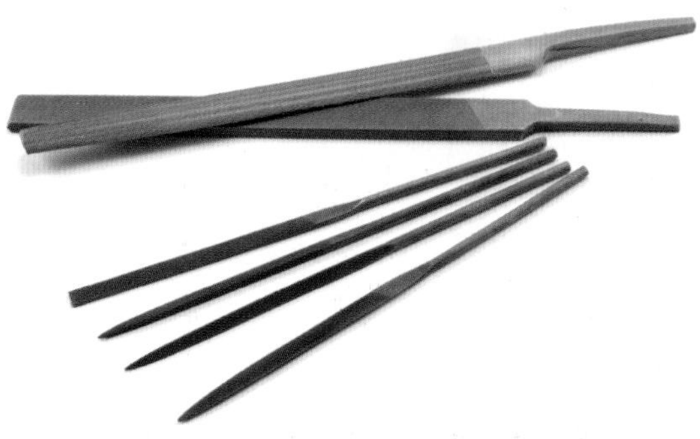

FILES A variety of file sizes, shapes, and cuts are used in this book, including heavy, half round, triangle, and flat. For most of the projects in this book, use a medium cut.

Shaping, Sizing, and Marking Tools

Shaping tools, such as a dapping block and bracelet bending pliers, will make you feel like a superhero, as you bend metal with ease! And sizing and marking tools will help ensure that the jewelry you create fits exactly as you wish.

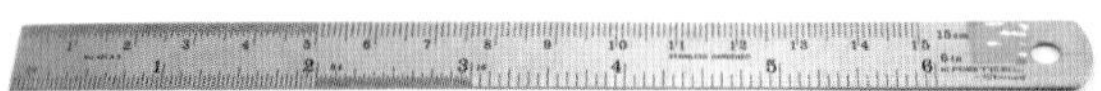

METAL JEWELER'S RULER This ruler is very accurate and provides a hard edge to work against.

TAPERED STEEL RING MANDREL A mandrel is used to measure the size of ring blanks. It's also useful as a support when stamping or hammering rings.

SCRIBE A scribe is a scratch tool for marking hard metal.

METAL DAPPING BLOCK AND ROUNDED PUNCHES This tool consists of a block with various-size wells and corresponding punches; use it to create domes from metal blanks.

BRACELET BENDING PLIERS The heads of this nylon-jaw tool are curved to help shape a cuff or bangle bracelet. Replacement heads are available if yours become worn.

Polishing Tools and Materials

Oxidizing and polishing stamped metal adds depth and beauty to the finished piece. These tools aid in finishing your jewelry to perfection.

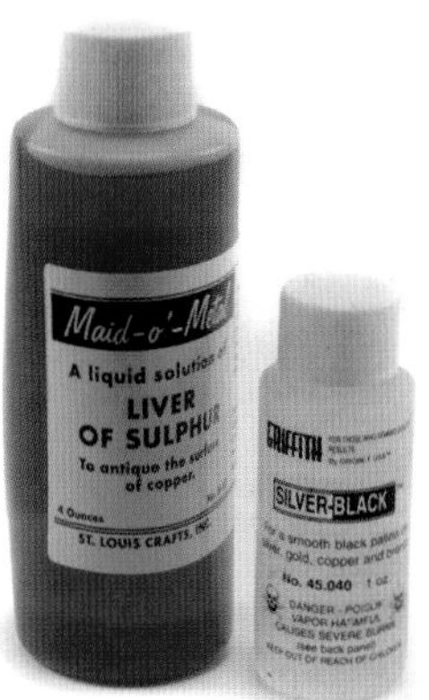

OXIDIZING SOLUTION Chemical oxidizing solutions are readily available. The most commonly used solutions are liver of sulfur and hydrochloric acid-based solutions, sold under brand names including Silver Black and Black Max. These solutions are caustic; use with care in a well-ventilated area. You may also darken the metal with black permanent marker or oxidize with a natural method using a hard-boiled egg. See page 30 for more information on oxidizing methods.

PRO POLISH PADS Look for polish pads with a bonded micro-abrasive, which allows the pads to remove oxidation and polish to a high-luster finish, doing the job of steel wool and a polish cloth in one step. Do not get these pads wet.

ADDITIONAL HELPFUL TOOLS

These tools are only required for one or two projects in this book; add them to your metalsmithing supply cabinet as you're able.

#0000 STEEL WOOL AND POLISHING CLOTH Steel wool and a polishing cloth can be used to remove oxidation. These can be found at any hardware or paint supply store.

NAIL BUFFER A four-sided nail buffer works well to smooth out rough file marks.

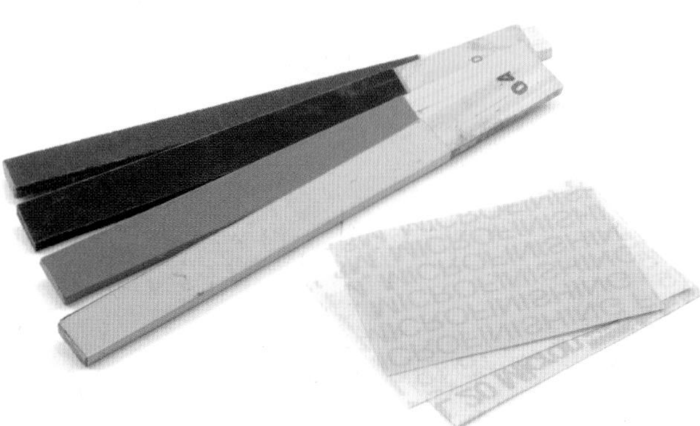

SANDPAPER AND SANDING STICKS Sandpaper and sanding sticks are useful for final finishing; these can also be found at hardware or paint supply stores.

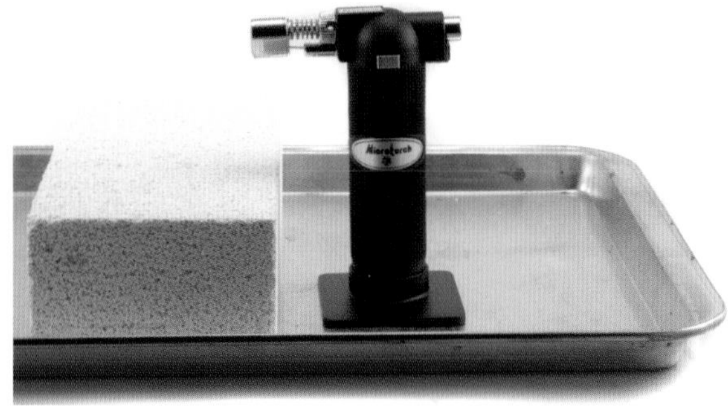

BUTANE TORCH AND KILN BRICK A small butane torch is useful for fusing or, in our case, annealing metal. Look for one at a jewelry supply house or even a kitchen supply store—they're also used to make crème brûlée. When using the torch, place a kiln brick—a lightweight, soft, insulating brick—under the metal while firing, and work on a metal tray or baking sheet. It's also important to have a fire extinguisher nearby.

TUMBLER I use a tumbler with mixed-shape steel shot and a cleaning/burnishing compound for cleaning, polishing, and hardening metal. After oxidizing and polishing metal, give it an hour or so in the tumbler for a high-polish finish. (If you "oxidized" with a permanent marker, however, the tumbler will cause that black to fade quickly.)

LEATHER HOLE PUNCH This is a multi-size hole punch made specifically for leather.

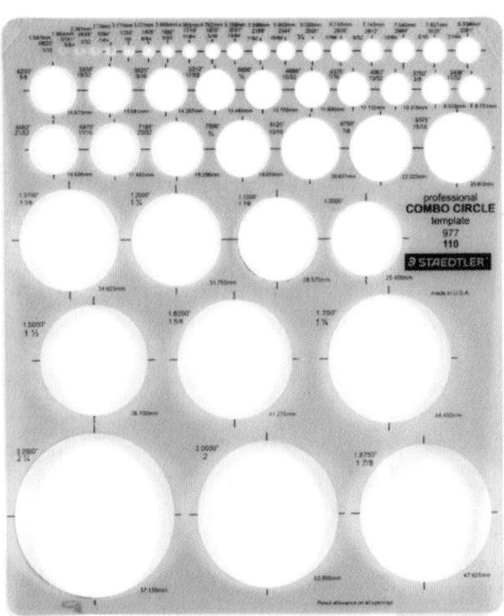

CIRCLE TEMPLATE This template has multi-size circles and guides on each circle; it is available at art supply stores and office supply stores.

SNAP SETTER SET The snap setter is a hand tool, used to set snaps, made for use with leather.

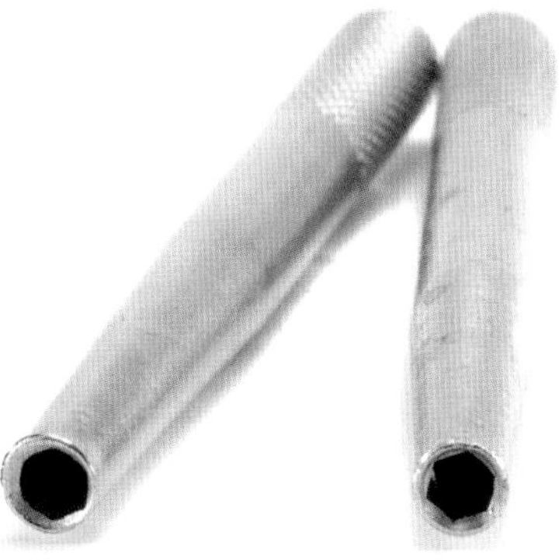

EZ SOCKET WRENCHES These wrenches are made for use with miniature hex-head bolts, making it easy to tighten the tiny nuts and bolts.

MATERIALS

Many precious metals and other metals are suitable for making stamped metal jewelry; the only rule is that the metal must be soft enough to take an impression. You can work with prefabricated shapes or create your own from sheet metal.

Prefabricated Shapes

You'll find a variety of prefabricated shapes on the market. These shapes, often referred to as blanks, are cut from sheet metal using a die, so the edges may be slightly sharp. File them lightly with a fine file or sandpaper, or let them roll around in a tumbler for an hour or so. The popularity of stamped jewelry is on the rise, so it's easy to find blanks in whimsical, traditional, unusual, and classical shapes, most commonly in 24-gauge thickness.

You may also find prefabricated shapes and components that have been cast rather than cut. These are often thicker than 24-gauge metal, with smooth, rounded edges that won't require filing.

Check your local jewelry supply store or bead store for precious-metal findings with blank spots suitable for stamping. You will be surprised by how many components you can find.

Sheet Metal

Don't limit yourself to prefabricated shapes! Challenge yourself by cutting your own shapes from sheet metal using a jeweler's saw or shears (see Cutting & Sawing, page 23).

Precious Metals Suitable for Stamping

Most people love to wear silver, gold, or gold-filled jewelry, for good reason; these precious metals have a beautiful sheen and a special beauty. They're well suited to stamping, so you can use them to your heart's content.

STERLING SILVER Sterling silver is an alloy of 92.5 percent silver and 7.5 percent of other metals, usually copper. You'll find the largest variety of prefabricated shapes in sterling silver.

FINE SILVER Fine silver is 99.9 percent pure silver. This metal is very soft, so you should lighten up your whack when stamping on this metal.

GOLD-FILLED Gold-filled metal has a layer of gold bonded onto a base metal, usually brass. The base-metal core is clad with 10 percent (by weight) 12k or 14k gold. This differs from gold plating, which is a light layer of gold rather than a heavy bonded layer. Gold-filled sheet metal is sold as single-clad or double-clad; single-clad has gold bonded to one side of the sheet, meant to be the decorative side, and double-clad has a layer of gold on both sides. I find that when stamping gold-filled metal, I can use the same force behind my hammer as I would with sterling silver.

LD Prefabricated shapes made from pure gold are more ited than those available in sterling silver or gold-filled tal; you may find only basic circles. You can certainly cut ır own shapes from gold sheet. Because gold is so ensive, I recommend the gold-filled metal as a high-quality ion. If you do stamp on gold, use a light whack as you would h fine silver, because gold is a very soft metal.

her Metals Suitable for Stamping

ile most of the projects in this book use precious metals for mping, other metals, such as copper and nickel, add design ions. For example, copper looks great combined with rling silver. There are a few metals to use with caution: minum sheet metal is available, but is very soft and must be mped lightly. You may also find steel prefabricated shapes, h as washers and keys. But steel is very hard and requires ch more force behind your hammer. Stamping on steel will rten the life of your stamps, especially inexpensive ones.

PPER Copper is fairly soft, inexpensive, and widely ilable; I use it often. You can find a wide variety of fabricated shapes in copper.

KEL SILVER Nickel silver is a metal alloy of 65 percent per, 18 percent nickel, and 17 percent zinc. It's named for silvery appearance but contains no true silver. Nickel silver old as sheet metal or in prefabricated shapes. Because ny people are sensitive to nickel and prefer not to wear elry made from it, I like to use this metal for keychain rms, plaques, and various other non-jewelry designs.

BASIC METALSMITHING TECHNIQUES

The metalsmithing techniques in this chapter are very compatible with stamped metal designs. They allow you to create beautiful jewelry for any occasion, as you texture, shape, join, and polish components with dazzling results. While these techniques are not difficult, you'll benefit from practicing and experimenting. Work carefully and safely, and you'll feel like a master metalsmith in no time.

HAMMERING & TEXTURING

The metals we work with in this book are all fairly soft, to better take the impression of a stamp. This also makes it easy to add texture to the metal, another attractive design element for jewelry. With a selection of stamps and hammers, you can make many kinds of textures.

Texturing with Stamps

Use letter, number, and design stamps to easily create texture. Expand your vision of these stamps; repeat them in a pattern, or stamp free-form. Letters can also create texture. For example, I frequently use an x stamp to create pattern. I also use the period stamp often, especially around the border of a blank. To texture with design stamps, simply stamp the design over and over again. Avoid letting the stamp overlap with another impression because this tends to blur the texture you are trying to create. **FIGURE 1** shows the stamps used to create the textured metal in **FIGURE 2**.

Texturing with Hammers

Hammers are also useful for texturing. Start looking at hammers with a new eye, seeing them not for their intended use but as a tool for texturing. Keep your eye out for hammers with interestingly shaped heads. Whenever texturing with hammers, remember to work with your metal on a bench block.

TEXTURE HAMMERS These hammers are produced specifically for texturing and have designs or patterns on the face **(FIGURE 3)**. They can be purchased readymade, or make one yourself by altering the surface of a regular household hammer by filing or carving. The design on the face will transfer to sheet metal or wire on your bench block as you strike it. Make patterns by striking overlapping blows on the metal to produce a pattern with a random effect.

FIGURE 1

RIVETING HAMMER The long, thin end of this hammer is great for adding a linear texture to your metal. Strike the hammer repeatedly at the same angle for a symmetrical pattern **(FIGURE 4)**.

For a crisscross pattern, strike the metal repeatedly after changing the angle of the hammer 90 degrees **(FIGURE 5)**.

CHASING HAMMER The ball end of a chasing hammer makes a dimpled surface on the metal. Strike your metal gently for a light, small dimpled effect **(FIGURE 6)** or strike hard for a deeper effect that resembles dots **(FIGURE 7)**.

Other Texturing Ideas

Although the projects in this book are textured with hammers, you can also transfer onto metal the pattern of any hard-textured surface, such as an open-mesh screen, a patterned brass sheet, or a shape made from hard wire. Lay the hard-textured surface on top of your sheet metal or wire and hammer the surface with a brass-head mallet or household hammer.

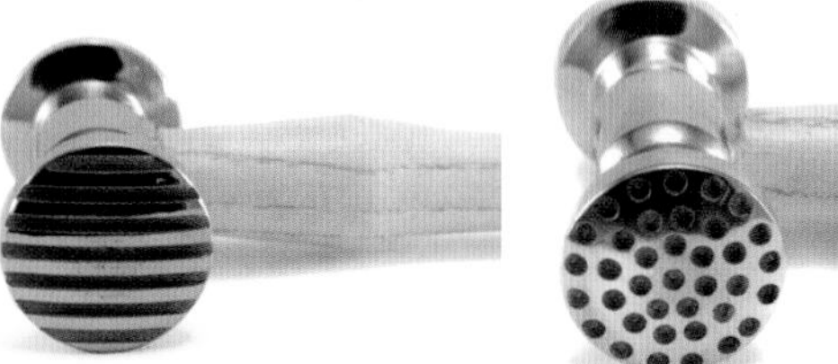

FIGURE 3

FIGURE 2

FIGURE 4

FIGURE 5

FIGURE 6

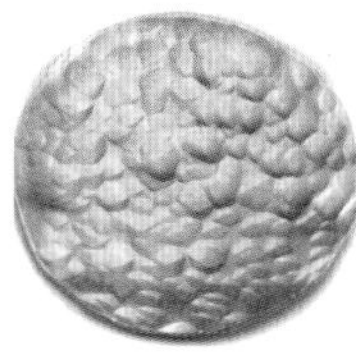

FIGURE 7

CUTTING & SAWING

Various tools are available to help you cut metal into almost any shape you can imagine. Choose the tool that is easiest to manipulate through the metal and that will give the smoothest and most precise cut. Jeweler's saws and metal shears work well for the projects in this book.

Transferring a Pattern

Before cutting a shape out of metal, you'll need to transfer a pattern to use as a guideline. Create a template from card stock or other heavy paper and trace around it with a permanent marker or a metal scribe. Transparent plastic templates, available at any craft store, are handy for drawing shapes such as circles and squares. Use a metal jeweler's ruler to measure and draw straight lines; these thin metal rulers have both imperial and metric measurements and are handy for precise measurements.

Choosing a Cutting Tool

After transferring the pattern to the metal, choose a cutting tool. A saw is perfect for cutting metal that is 26- to 16-gauge. Shears work well on thinner gauges, from 22-gauge all the way to 30-gauge. It's difficult to get a saw through thinner gauges (28-gauge and above) because the metal has a tendency to move around during the sawing process. Shears cut through thinner sheets more quickly and easily.

METAL SHEARS Shears come in different styles, including the French spring shear and the scissors shear. Both of these styles have heavy metal blades that cut like a regular pair of scissors. Look for blades that are smooth on the edges so the cut will also be smooth.

JEWELER'S SAW A jeweler's saw is comprised of a frame and blades. The saw frame is adjustable—the opening can be made wider or narrower according to preference. Blades come in a variety of sizes. Choose the blade size according to the gauge of metal. The most useful sizes for the projects in this book are:

- 2/0 with 56.0 teeth per 1" (2.5 cm) for 20- to 22-gauge metal
- 4/0 with 66 teeth per 1" (2.5 cm) for 22- to 24-gauge metal

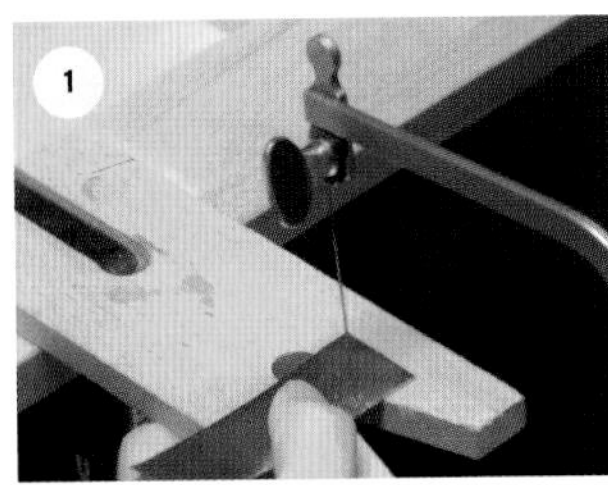

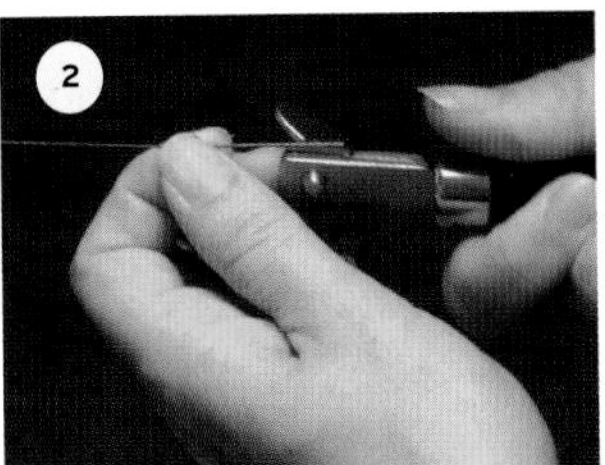

When sawing, do not bear down too heavily on the saw frame; this will cause the teeth to bind in the metal and make the saw impossible to use. Apply cut lube to the sides of the blades and the surface of the project for further ease of sawing. Use a light touch and saw with short up-and-down strokes with the saw placed at a 90-degree angle to the work **(FIGURE 1)**.

When turning a corner, you may be tempted to turn your saw. This could result in snapping the blade. Instead, saw in place as you turn the metal.

To insert a saw blade into the frame:

1 Open both the top and bottom clamps by unscrewing the thumbscrew. Insert the blade, with the teeth facing down and out, into the top clamp and tighten.

2 Next, hold the saw with the handle against your body and the head of the frame braced on a stable table. Push the frame against the table, causing the frame to bow, while inserting the blade into the bottom clamp **(FIGURE 2)**.

3 Tighten the bottom thumbscrew and release the tension. When you pluck the blade, you should hear a nice high ping.

SAW BLADE SIZE GUIDE

GAUGE OF METAL	SIZE OF SAW BLADE
16	2, 3, OR 4
18	1 OR 2
20	1/0 OR 2/0
22	2/0 OR 3/0
24	3/0 OR 4/0
26	5/0 OR 6/0

HOLE PUNCHING & DRILLING

Learning to make smooth, accurate holes in metal will help you to rivet and link shapes with ease. Holes can be punched or drilled. These are my favorite tools.

Hole-Punch Pliers

Using a pair of hole-punch pliers is the fastest and easiest way to pop a hole in metal. These pliers work best with metal that is 20-gauge and thinner. Hole-punch pliers come in various sizes, and some have replaceable pins in case they become dull or break. When using these pliers, place a piece of plastic mesh or a polish pad as padding between the pliers and the metal piece **(FIGURE 1)**.

Hole-punch pliers are perfect for punching a hole at the edge of metal, but the size of the head of the pliers limits their reach. For best results, use a permanent marker to mark the placement of the hole on the metal before punching.

Screw-Down Hole Punch

The screw-down hole punch is similar to hole-punch pliers, but it punches up to 14-gauge metal. Instead of making the hole by squeezing the pliers, the screw-down hole punch has a screw mechanism that you twist down through the metal to make the hole **(FIGURE 2)**.

The screw-down hole punch has two different hole sizes. One side measures 1.6 mm and fits up to 14-gauge wire, and the other is 2.3 mm, fitting up to 12-gauge wire. The twist mechanism is replaceable if the stem breaks. Again, the size of the tool limits the placement of holes.

Drills

A power tool, such as a Dremel rotary tool or a flexible-shaft tool, gives you more options with the placement and the size of a hole than do pliers or a hole punch. These tools require more safety precautions, however. Always wear eye protection when using a drill and wear protective gloves or hold the metal with a ring clamp so as not to burn your hands as the metal piece heats up during drilling.

1 Choose the correct size drill bit for the hole you want to make and insert it into the Dremel or flex-shaft tool. Make sure that the bit is inserted tightly into the tool. Apply a bit of cut lube by turning on the tool and quickly inserting the tip into the lubricant to coat the drill bit.

2 Stamp a center punch into your metal to mark the placement of the hole **(FIGURE 3)**. The center punch will form a dip in the metal and provide a stable place for the bit to sit when you begin drilling.

3 Place a block of soft wood under the piece to be drilled so that the drill bit will have a surface to drill through after piercing the metal **(FIGURE 4)**. When drilling, apply steady, even pressure. Use a needle file or bead reamer to remove any burrs that remain after the hole is drilled.

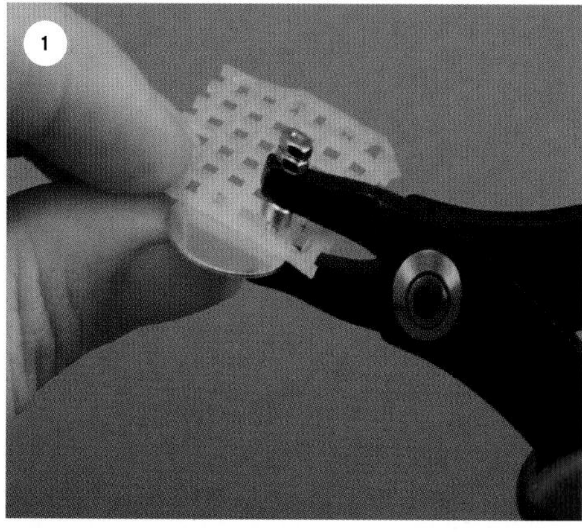

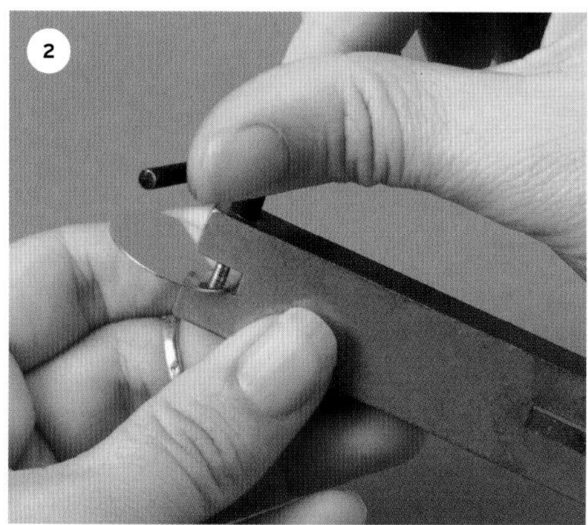

DRILL-BIT GUIDE

SIZE OF HOLE BY GAUGE	SIZE OF HOLE IN INCHES	SIZE OF HOLE IN MILLIMETERS	DRILL BIT SIZE
20	.0320"	.8128 mm	67
18	.0403"	1.0236 mm	60
16	.0508"	1.2903 mm	55
14	.0641"	1.6281 mm	51 or 52
12	.0808"	2.0523 mm	46

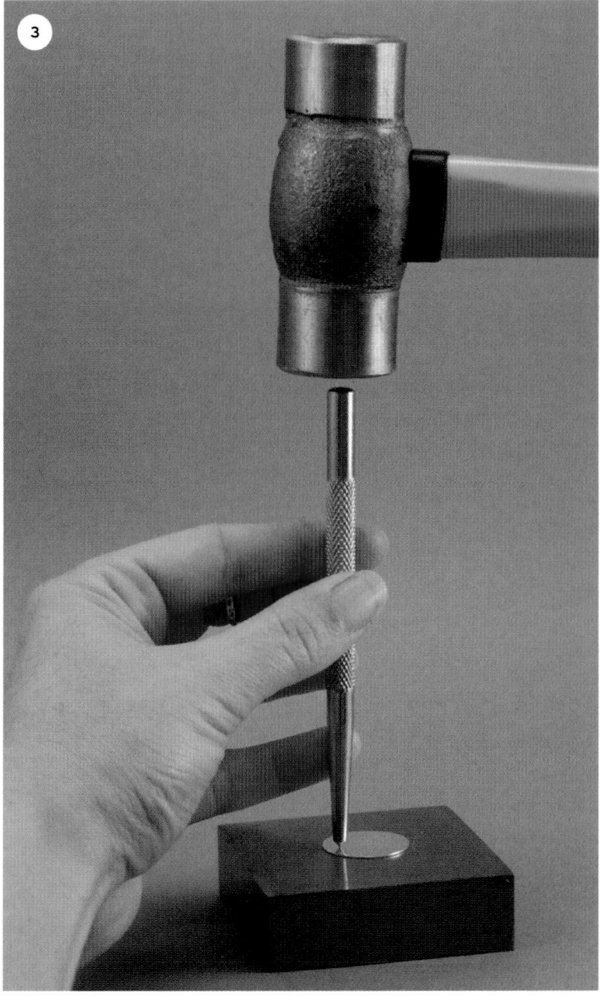

DAPPING

Dapping is a method of hammering a metal disc into a dome, using a metal block with depressions of various sizes and rounded dapping punches in corresponding sizes. Use a 1-pound brass hammer to strike the punches.

How to Dap

Complete any stamping or holes before dapping. When sizing holes for a domed piece, note that the hole will enlarge about one gauge size after dapping depending on how much the final dome is curved. The hole may be enlarged after dapping by filing with a round needle file, diamond-tipped bead reamer bit, or drill.

When dapping a blank that has been stamped, place the blank design-side down in the well of the block, and use lighter blows to strike the punch so as not to remove the design.

1 Place the metal blank into a shallow depression in the block **(FIGURE 1)**.

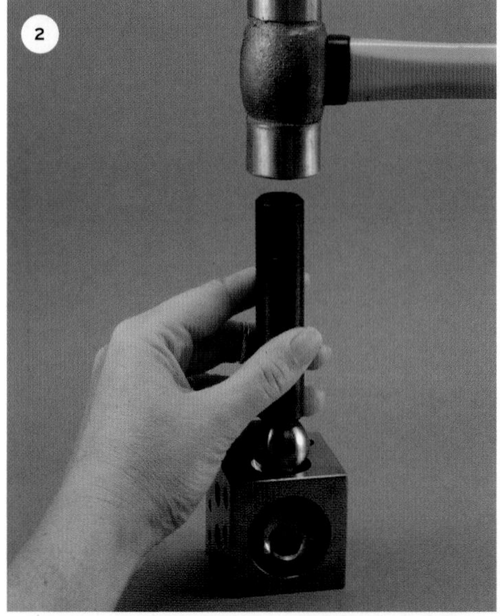

2 Choose a punch that fits snugly into the depression and tap lightly with the hammer **(FIGURE 2)**.

3 The punch will rotate slightly in the depression as you shape the metal. Use light repetitive strikes to gradually form the dome **(FIGURE 3)**.

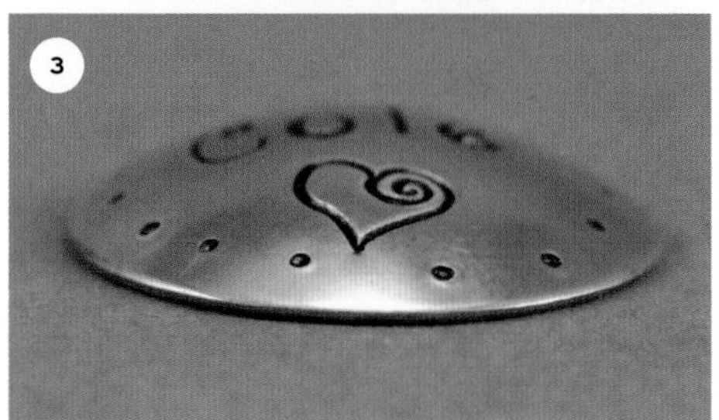

4 If a more pronounced dome is desired, move the blank to a deeper well in the block and repeat the process.

Take care not to strike the edges of the blank, because this will cause them to become uneven. If this happens, file the edges flush using a flat file.

RIVETING

Riveting is a process of connecting two pieces of metal together without soldering and also adds a design element to the project. Projects in this book use wire rivets and tube rivets.

Wire Rivet

Riveting with wire (referred to as a standard rivet) is a relatively simple technique.

1 Drill holes of equal size in the two pieces of metal you want to attach, using the chart on page 25 to determine the correct drill bit size for the wire's gauge. The rivet wire must fit snugly in the drilled hole. It's best to make the hole slightly smaller than the gauge of wire; the hole can then be enlarged slightly with a round needle file to ensure a nice tight fit. If the wire is loose, riveting will be difficult, because the wire will move around in the hole and be hard to strike, and it will not properly flare out.

2 Insert the wire into the holes and mark the cutting line with a permanent marker. Cut using flush cutters, leaving about 1 mm to 1.5 mm on either side **(FIGURE 1)**. A longer wire will result in a rivet with a larger head.

3 Place the metal, with the rivet inserted, on a bench block and file the top of the wire if needed **(FIGURE 2)**. The wire should be perfectly flat before beginning the rivet.

4 Tap the rivet head with the long, thin end of a riveting hammer. Tap lightly across the head of the rivet and rotate the piece 45 degrees. Continue to tap and turn until a full rotation is completed. Turn the piece over and repeat on the other side. The head of the wire will begin to form a mushroom shape and flare at the tip **(FIGURES 3 AND 4)**.

5 After both sides of the rivet are tapped out, use the flat side of the riveting hammer to further widen and smooth the rivet head. Repeat on both sides until the rivet is the desired size **(FIGURE 5)**.

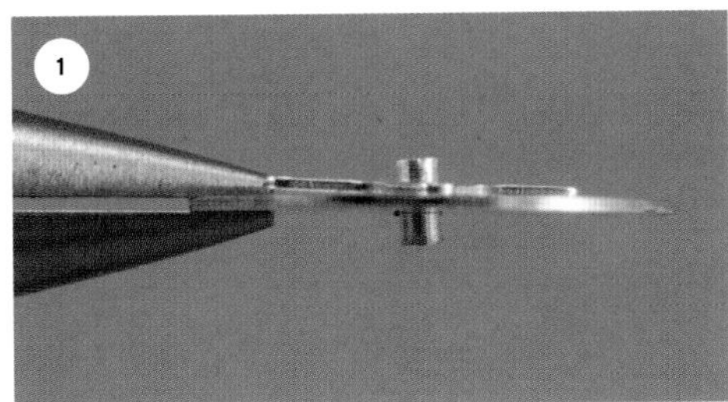

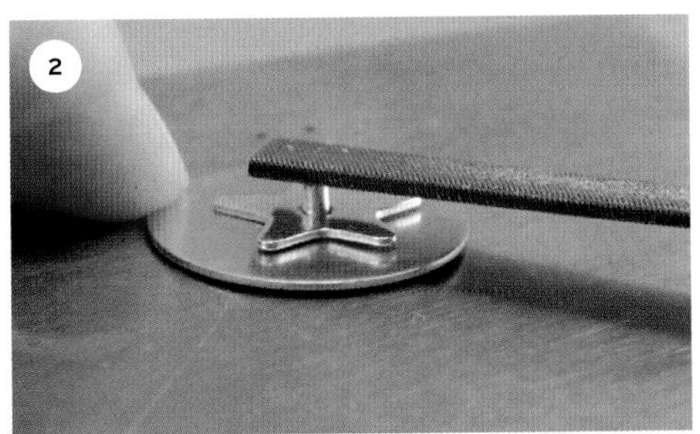

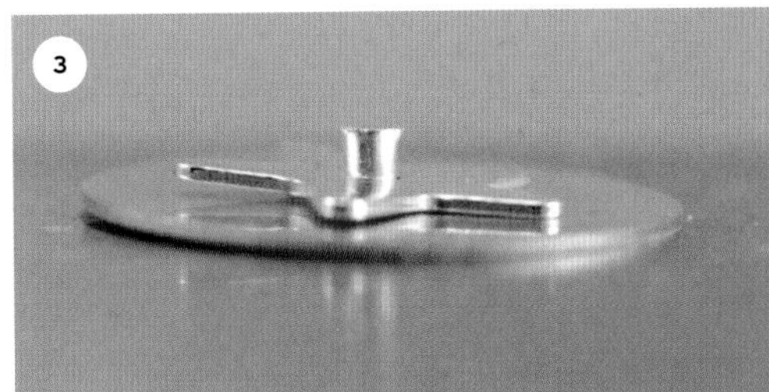

Nailhead Rivet

There are times when you'll need to build a rivet head before inserting it into metal, such as the Stamped & Stacked Ring project on page 68. This is sometimes called a nailhead rivet.

1 Clamp the wire in a table vice with plastic or rubber covers on the clamps. Allow the wire to protrude only ⅛" (2 mm).

2 Clamp very tightly on the wire so it will not move when it is hammered. Slightly hammer the tip of the wire with the long end of the riveting hammer **(FIGURE 6)**.

3 Tap lightly in one direction, then change your position 90 degrees and continue to tap until the tip mushrooms out.

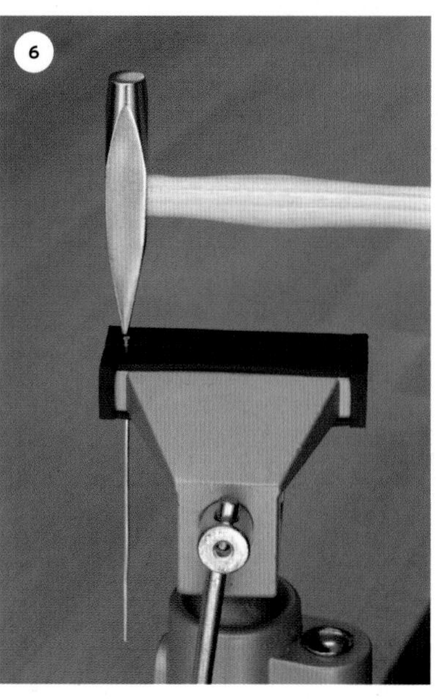

HOLE SIZES IN GAUGE, INCHES & MILLIMETERS

GAUGE	INCHES	MILLIMETERS
12	.081"	2.05 mm
14	.064"	1.62 mm
16	.051"	1.29 mm
18	.040"	1.02 mm
20	.032"	.812 mm

Tube Rivet

Tube riveting uses hollow tube rather than solid wire to connect the metal pieces together. The tube shouldn't extend more than 1 mm on either side of the two metal pieces. If the tube is too long, it will split when riveted. Follow this process to make a tube rivet.

1 Drill holes.

2 Measure and mark the cutting line for the tube as for a standard rivet but use a jeweler's saw to cut the tube so that it will not collapse or pinch closed at the end. For ease of cutting, use metal-tube-cutting pliers to hold the tube and a 4/0 saw blade in a jeweler's saw frame.

3 To saw, insert the tube into the section of the cutting pliers that grips the tube most firmly. This is usually the smallest section in the pliers. The cutting line should show in the gap in the head of the jaws **(FIGURE 7)**. Apply cut lube to the saw blade. Hold the pliers with the tube in your nondominant hand while sawing the tube with your dominant hand. Saw through using light up-and-down strokes **(FIGURE 8)**.

4 If a tube-cutting pliers is not available, you'll need a raised surface such as a bench pin or bench block to stabilize the tube for cutting. Place the tube on the raised surface, with the marked area to be cut hanging over the side. Hold the tube firmly with your nondominant hand and saw with your dominant hand. Be careful to keep your fingers out of the way when sawing **(FIGURE 9)**.

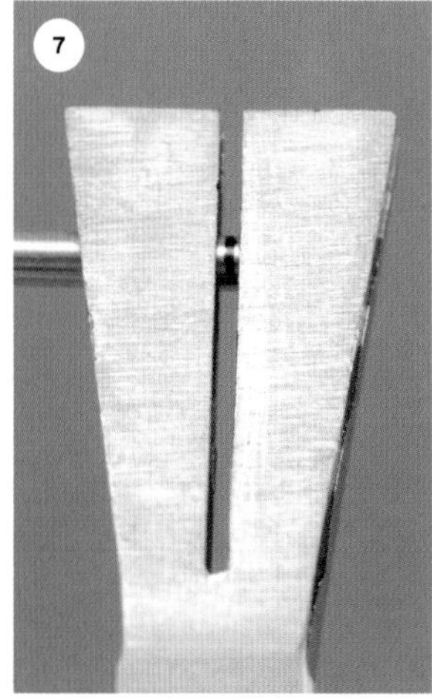

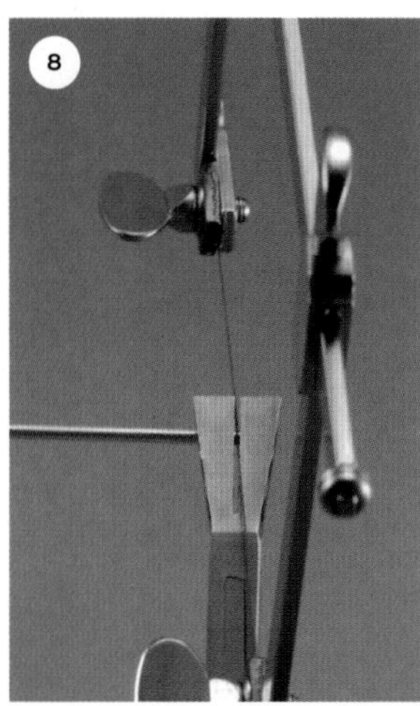

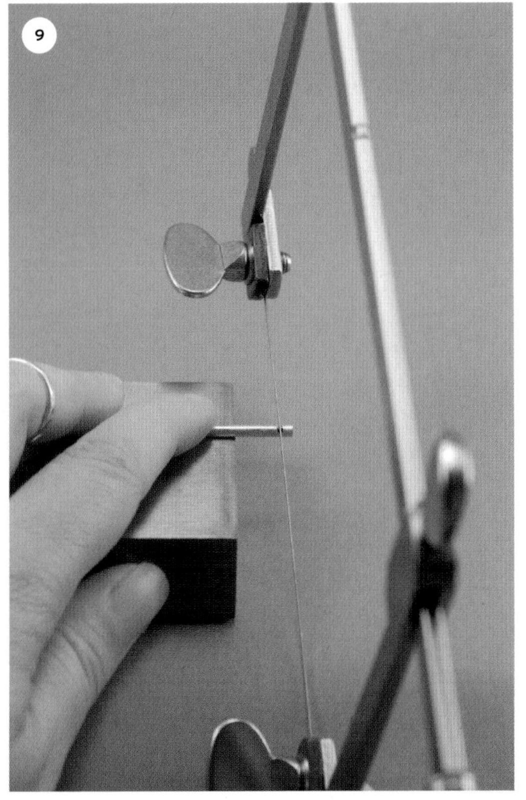
9

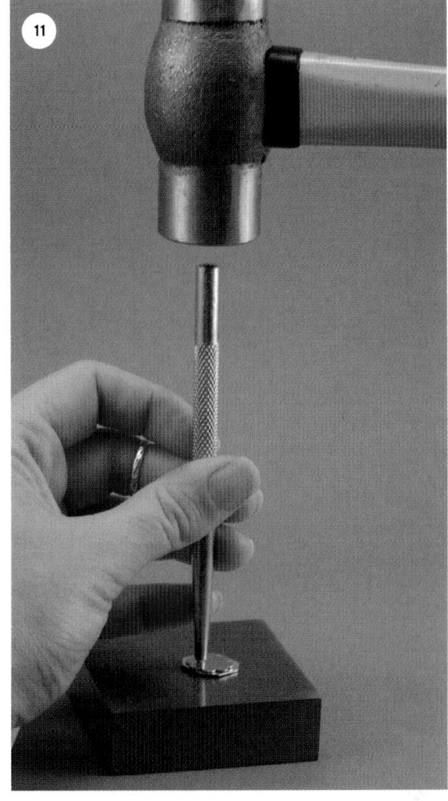
11

10

12

5 Insert the tube into the piece to be riveted and place a center punch in the hole of the tube **(FIGURE 10)**.

6 Tap the center punch lightly with a 1-pound brass hammer **(FIGURE 11)** while rotating the punch slightly so that the edges of the tube begin to flare out **(FIGURE 12)**. Turn the piece over and repeat on the other side.

7 Switch to the flat head of the riveting hammer and tap the edges of the tube rivet flat and smooth on both sides **(FIGURE 13)**.

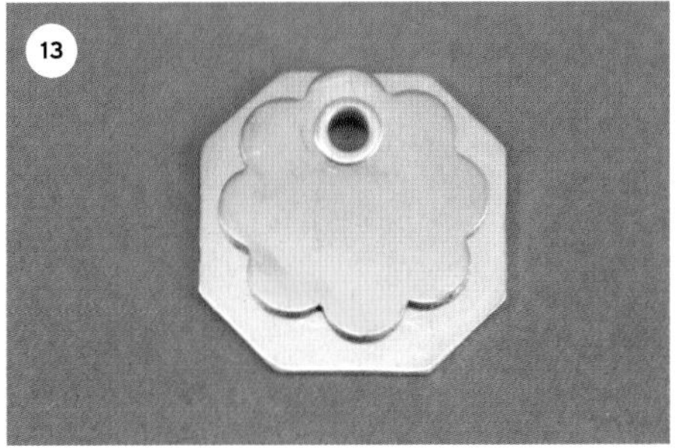
13

OXIDIZING & POLISHING

Oxidizing and polishing stamped metal adds contrast to the impressions, making designs stand out and words easier to read. **FIGURES 1** and **2** illustrate a stamped shape before and after oxidizing and polishing.

Oxidizing Methods

To oxidize metal, I use one of the two oxidizing agents described below. These solutions react with metal, causing a gray or blackish effect on the surface. I've also included two other methods that you can explore.

Please wear gloves and work in a well-ventilated area when applying oxidizing agents. Make sure the metal is clean; grease, oil, or permanent pen marks will act as a resist. Always store oxidizing agents in an airtight container, in a cool, dark place, away from tools or metal supplies.

LIVER OF SULFUR Liver of sulfur (LOS) is a mixture of potassium sulfides and is available in liquid and chunk forms. The fumes are harmful, and they smell really horrible, so it's essential to work in a well-ventilated area, preferably outside.

1 Mix a small amount of LOS in hot (not boiling) water and work in small batches. If using the chunk form of LOS, dilute one pea-size piece in 1 to 2 cups (237 to 474 ml) of water. If using the liquid concentrate, use 1 teaspoon (5 ml) per 4 cups (946 ml) of water.

2 Metal takes a patina best if it is hot; immerse the metal in hot water before putting it in the LOS bath.

3 Remove the metal from the hot water bath using chopsticks, a plastic utensil, or a gloved hand, and place it in the LOS bath.

4 Leave the metal in the solution, flipping or stirring with a nonmetal utensil (such as a plastic spoon) if necessary, to cover all of the metal.

5 It will take 30 seconds to a few minutes to achieve the very deep gray of full oxidation **(FIGURE 3)**. Remove the metal from the LOS bath and rinse it thoroughly under cold water.

6 Follow the polishing directions below.

An LOS solution works well on fine silver, sterling silver, bronze, and copper. Copper darkens much faster than sterling does, so either make a weaker solution or don't leave it in as long. This solution also works on gold-filled metal, but the metal must be as hot as possible when it enters the LOS bath.

HYDROCHLORIC ACID SOLUTIONS Hydrochloric acid (HCl) solution goes by different brand names, including Silver Black, Black Max, and Black Magic. This solution is much more toxic than liver of sulfur if it contacts skin or if the fumes are inhaled, so please use extra caution.

Use this solution in its concentrated form; there is no need to mix it with water. Unlike liver of sulfur, you do not need to soak your metal in it for any length of time; oxidation is instant. You can dip your metal in and out, and it will turn black. For me, the intense reaction with the metal is a bit much, and if I am oxidizing a large piece of jewelry, I prefer liver of sulfur. But for stamping, HCl solutions are great. For stamped pieces, oxidation is applied only to the impressions made by the letters and design stamps. To oxidize with an HCl solution, follow these steps:

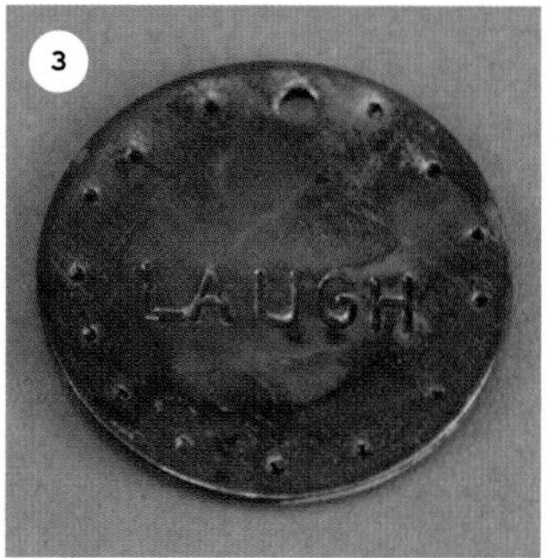

1 Hold the metal in a gloved hand.

2 Dip the tip of a cotton swab into the Silver Black (or other HCl solution) and dab it into the impressions in your metal. Push the tip of the cotton swab down hard so the solution really sinks in. Rinse immediately with cold water.

3 Follow the polishing directions below.

HCl solution works well on fine silver and sterling silver. It is not recommended for copper or gold-filled metal.

PERMANENT PEN Use permanent ink for a quick and easy way to put black in stamped impressions. Just use a permanent pen and push the tip down hard while drawing over the letters or designs. Polish as you normally would. The ink will fade after a while and will need to be touched up.

BOILED-EGG METHOD (THE AU NATURALE WAY) Hard-boil an egg. While it's still hot or warm, smash the egg with the shell on and put the entire crushed egg and shells in a zip-top plastic bag or small container, along with your stamped metal. The older and more "expired" the egg, the better the coloration. Flip or shake the bag to ensure that all the metal darkens and leave the bag for 1 to 3 hours. Rinse the metal and polish following the directions below.

Polishing

Once your metal is black (or, more accurately, dark gray), polish the surface so that the patina remains only in the impressions. I like to use polish pads, often sold as Pro Polish Pads. These pretreated squares contain a micro-abrasive and a polishing agent that remove black from the surface of metal while giving it a high shine.

Another popular method is to use very fine #0000 steel wool and a polishing cloth. Buff the metal with the steel wool to remove the color from the surface. Follow up with a polishing cloth for a nice shine finish. Steel wool can sometimes leave a slightly brushed look. If you like the brushed look, use coarser steel wool or a steel brush.

OPTIONAL If you have a tumbler, toss your polished metal into it along with some steel shot and a few drops of Dawn liquid detergent for a final high-shine mirror finish.

ANNEALING

Annealing in metalwork is a method of softening metal after it has been work-hardened. Work-hardening occurs when metal is hammered or shaped repeatedly, or when it is fabricated. For example, flat wire or regular round wire can be harder than expected simply due to hardening during fabrication, and you may need to anneal, or soften, the wire to properly bend or shape it.

If you're stamping a metal that is too hard to take an impression well, annealing the metal will soften it for better results. To anneal:

1 Protect your worktable with a thin sheet of metal.

2 Place the metal to be annealed on a kiln brick or other soldering surface and heat gradually with a butane torch until the metal emits a dull red glow **(FIGURE 1)**. Maintain that temperature for about a minute or so and then remove the torch.

3 It's best to let the metal cool naturally, but if you're in a hurry, quench it by dropping it into cool water in a metal bowl.

4 The metal is now softened and ready for further work.

Copper and sterling silver (which is made with a small percentage of copper) are both metals that produce fire scale, a layer of dark gray oxidation, when heated. For the projects in this book, I recommend removing fire scale by buffing the metal with steel wool until all traces of the oxidation are removed. (If working with fine silver, no copper is present in the metal and therefore no fire scale is produced during heating.)

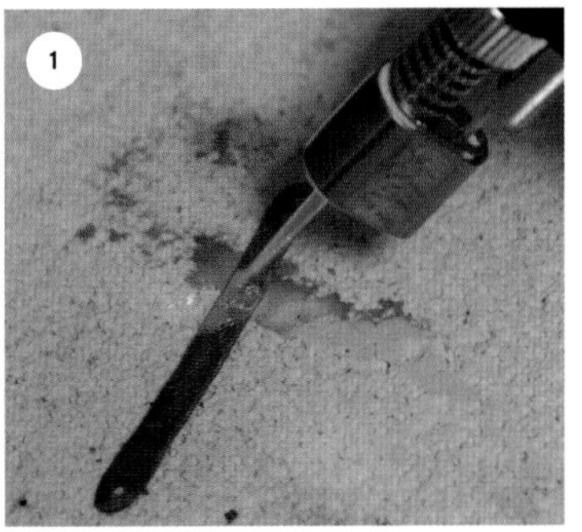

Basic Stamped Pendant, variations

GETTING STARTED
STAMPING

Over many years of working with metal, I've developed some tried-and-true ways of bringing stamped words and designs to life in jewelry. In this chapter, I share those stamping techniques with you. We begin with a review of important safety guidelines for stamping and other jewelry-making activities.

SAFETY FIRST!

A variety of tools and materials are used in making jewelry, and taking a few precautions and learning the ins and outs of your tools and materials will be helpful along the way. Carefully follow the precautions below, and remember, safety first.

An organized workstation is a safe workstation. Store your tools and equipment properly to ensure that they last for years, as well as to prevent accidents. With everything in its place, you will have more time to create jewelry instead of using it to hunt for what you need.

Safety Glasses

Always wear safety glasses when stamping, as well as whenever you're using wire cutters, drilling, sawing, torching, or doing any technique that may pose a hazard to the eyes.

Gloves

Wear disposable protective gloves when using an oxidizing solution to prevent contact with the skin.

Acids

Some oxidizing solutions are caustic. A couple of tablespoons of baking soda in the rinse water will neutralize any remaining acid on the metal. Pour baking soda onto any spills that occur. Wipe with paper towels and discard.

Drilling

Drilling through metal and beads produces a fine dust; to prevent inhaling, wear a dust mask. Dip the metal or beads in water occasionally during drilling to help prevent the dust from entering the air.

Sawing

Be mindful of fingers when sawing. It's easy to get a momentum going and not pay attention to how close the blade is to your fingers. Saw blades have a tendency to snap after repeated use; applying cut lube to the blade will reduce breakage and will allow the blade to move through the metal more quickly and easily.

Using a Butane Torch

Always wear safety glasses, pull your hair back, wear natural fibers, and work in a well-ventilated area. Have a fire extinguisher nearby. Use a proper fire-safe work surface when using a torch; a thin sheet of metal or an old baking sheet or pan is perfect for this purpose. The torch tip will be hot after using, so take care not to burn yourself after the torch has been extinguished. Keep a cooling cup and tweezers nearby to quench hot metals.

SET UP YOUR WORK SPACE

Setting up a clean, organized work space, with safety and comfort in mind, will make your stamping and jewelry-making experience positive and fun! Follow these tips for success.

- Work on a strong, stable table for good stamping results. A wobbly or weak table will absorb some of the impact of the stamp and result in a weak impression. Avoid placing your table on a really thick rug. If you're working on a fairly strong table but you need a bit more resistance, position your bench block directly over a table leg.

- Work under good lighting. Good lighting helps you better line up your stamps and evenly space each character.

- Always work on a steel bench block. The resistance of hardened metal under your fine metal ensures a nice deep impression.

- Make sure any clamped tools are securely fastened to your bench or table. In this book, we work with a bench vise and a V-slot bench pin. Make sure both are tightly screwed to the table so that they don't wiggle at all.

- Keep your stamps organized. Good-quality letter sets come in wooden boxes with a slot for each stamp. Keep them alphabetized, replacing each letter after use, to save searching time. Keep your design stamps in a piece of wood with holes drilled to accommodate each stamp and with the designs facing up. This will save you time and frustration.

- Keep your tools clean and dry. Most of the stamping tools that you'll be working with are made from steel and can rust if exposed to moisture. If you live in a humid area or close to the ocean, you may notice rust on your tools or stamps that occurs just from exposure to the air. If rust does appear, buff with a little WD40 oil and fine steel wool to remove the rust. The steel will stay dark, but the rust will be removed and your tools will be as good as new!

- Take breaks and stretch! Always remember to take breaks and stretch your wrists, fingers, and shoulders—I once blew my wrist out doing production stamping work. Don't make the mistake of sitting at your table too long. Get up and walk around, get a glass of water, and stretch.

START STAMPING

Now that your work space is all set up and you're familiar with stamping tools and materials, let's stamp some jewelry! Stamping on metal is pretty straightforward, but there are some key tips that will really help you achieve impressive impressions. First, practice just hitting the stamp, then work on alignment. For practice, always work on a cheap piece of metal. Practice on a square of 24- to 20-gauge copper sheet.

The DVD enclosed with this book will also help you to see stamping in action and to visualize and understand the process. I hope you'll feel as if I'm right there to guide you as you begin to make stamped metal jewelry.

Basic Stamping

1 Make sure you are working on a steel bench block with a heavy hammer.

2 Pick up a letter stamp and hold it in your stabilizing hand. Hold the hammer in your dominant hand. I prefer to hold the hammer midway down the handle; holding it at the very end of the handle makes it harder to control.

3 Make sure the stamp is straight, perpendicular to the bench block, and perpendicular to the metal surface to be stamped. Press the stamp lightly into the metal.

4 Strike the stamp with your hammer. Make sure the hammer head comes down straight, parallel to the bench block, striking the stamp dead center **(FIGURE 1)**. If you hit off-center with the hammer, you will only impress that side of the letter.

5 Stamp that letter over and over again. Hit it once, move the stamp to a new spot on the metal, and stamp it again, to familiarize yourself with the amount of force you need behind the hammer to get an even and clear impression. It's okay to hammer the stamp more than once, but make sure that your stabilizing hand does not move at all.

6 If you stamp the letter with too little force, it won't be readable, and the oxidation step will polish out the impression. If you stamp it with too much force, you will most likely pick up the edge of your stamp in the metal and have a marred corner to the side of your letter. **FIGURE 2** shows a letter that was stamped with too little force, then too much, then the right amount.

Alignment

Now that you have the striking down, let's work on alignment—getting your letters in a straight line with the proper spacing between them. Still practicing on your copper sheet, draw a straight line on your metal. Stamp your letter several times and aim to get the letters in a straight line. It's not as easy as it looks! The letters are not always perfectly centered on the stamp, so lining up the shank of the stamp won't help—instead, look at each letter before stamping it.

Here are a few more tricks:

- Use a soft cloth to polish your metal so it is nice and shiny.
- Bring your stamp down to the metal, watching for the reflection of the letter in the metal. Lay the stamp down and then tip it to the left, leaving the left side of the stamp still in contact with the metal **(FIGURE 3)**. Peek under the stamp to make sure it is exactly where you want it. Tilt the letter back down and then strike it. This is the method that works best for me to line up my letters.

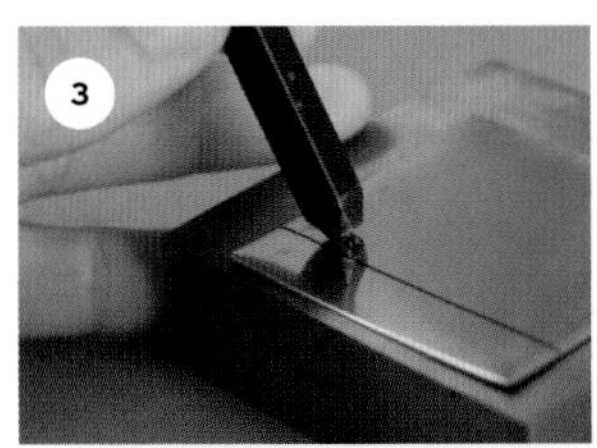

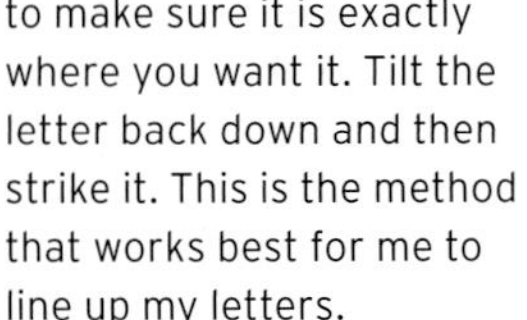

- Alternatively, tape the metal to the bench block with painter's tape. Create a guideline for the letters by placing the edge of the tape where you want the bottom of your letters to line up **(FIGURE 4)**. Place the stamp on the metal and lightly

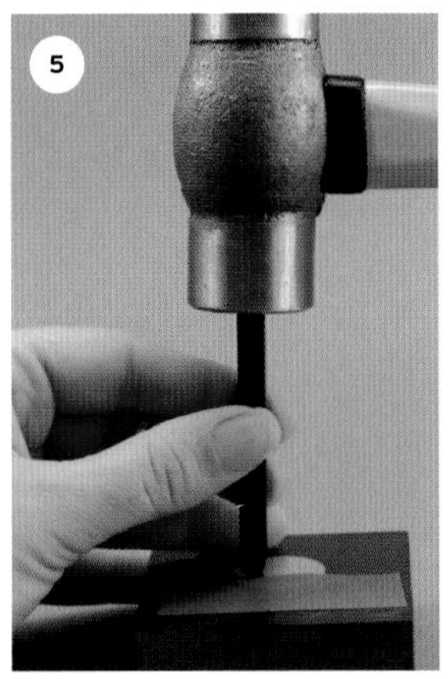

slide it down until you feel the bottom of the letter bump up against the edge of the tape and then strike the stamp **(FIGURE 5)**.

These are my tried-and-true methods, but the only way to perfect your alignment skills is to practice, practice, practice!

Centering Words

To center words on metal, first write out the word and assign a number to each letter. Find the center letter in your word and find the center of your blank and start stamping there. Then stamp out to the right and back to the left.

For example, if I were stamping the word *believe* on a 1" (2.5 cm) circle blank, I would start by stamping *i* in the dead center of that circle. From there, I would stamp *eve* to the right and then *l* to the left of the *i*, then *e* to the left of the *l*, and finally the *b*. It can be tricky spelling backward, so be sure to refer back to your written word.

For a longer piece—perhaps a saying that you want to stamp onto a cuff—write out the entire saying and assign numbers. Use two numbers for each space between words and the appropriate amount of numbers for any design stamps. Some design stamps are longer than others and may need to be assigned two numbers. Find the very center of the saying and start by stamping that letter in the center of your cuff.

Stamping with Design Stamps

Working with design stamps is a bit trickier than working with letters. The more design to the stamp, the harder it is to get a good impression. We are not removing metal when we stamp, we are moving it, so all that metal needs to move evenly.

Some tips for working with design stamps:

- Every design stamp has its own personality, so when you get a new one, make sure you practice with it before stamping on precious metals.

- Make sure there is absolutely no padding under your bench block. That padding will absorb some of the blow and will give your design a shadowed look. In **FIGURE 6**, I stamped the flower on the left with a folded dish towel under my bench block, resulting in a shadowed impression. For the flower on the right, I removed the towel and placed the block directly on the table—the impression is perfect.

- Make sure you are working on a stable table. A wobbly table, or a table on a thick carpet, will bounce and absorb some of the impact.

Tilt 'n Tap Method

If you are still struggling with a design stamp, consider using my Tilt 'n Tap method:

1 Hold the stamp steady in your stabilizing hand, pressing it lightly into the metal. Hit it once with your hammer.

2 Without moving or shifting the stamp, tilt it slightly to the right and strike it again.

3 Now tilt it slightly to the right and toward yourself a bit, then strike it again.

4 Continue in this manner, changing the angle of the tilt each time and moving in a circular motion until your last tilt is slightly away from you. You will be most successful with a total of six to eight tilts and taps (strikes).

Do not tilt the stamp too far, or you will stamp the edge of the stamp into the metal.

Also, don't hit the stamp too hard with each tilt. With other techniques you'd strike the stamp with one hard blow, but when using the Tilt 'n Tap method, a medium-hard strike works best.

EASY STAMPED
PENDANT

Stamped pendants are all the rage! You can find blanks in a variety of metals, shapes, thicknesses, and styles or cut your own custom shapes from sheet metal with metal shears or a jeweler's saw. These instructions are for an elegant single stamped circle, but the design options are as endless as your creativity.

TECHNIQUES

HOLE PUNCHING P. 24
DAPPING (OPTIONAL) P. 26
OXIDIZING & POLISHING P. 30
STAMPING P. 36

MATERIALS

Metal blank of your choice

Jump ring, 18-gauge, 4mm inner diameter

TOOLS

Letter/number stamp set and/or design stamps

Bench block

Safety glasses

Stamping hammer

Permanent marker

Hole-punch pliers, screw-down hole punch, or drill and drill bits

Oxidizing solution

Pro Polish polishing pads or #0000 steel wool and polishing cloth

Chain-nose pliers

A second pair of chain-nose or flat-nose pliers to aid in opening and closing jump ring

Metal dapping block (optional)

Plastic or rawhide mallet (optional)

FINISHED SIZE

Pendant size can vary from tiny to large and bold.

TIPS & TRICKS

- **If stamping or texturing begins to dome or distort your blank, hammer it flat with a plastic or rawhide mallet on a bench block.**
- **Use a period stamp or any small design stamp to stamp a border around the edge of your blank.**

EASY STAMPED PENDANTS

1 Write out the words you wish to stamp. If you are unsure whether your word will fit on your blank, stamp it first on some cheap sheet metal and measure it. Or you can press the stamps into a thick paper and measure it **(FIGURE 1)**.

2 Center your word and/or designs on the metal blank on the bench block, following the instructions on page 37. Put on your safety glasses and stamp using a stamping hammer.

3 Decide where to place your hole and mark the spot with a permanent marker. Punch the hole with a hole-punch pliers, screw-down hole punch, or drill and drill bit.

4 Oxidize and polish the blank.

5 If you want a slightly domed shape to the pendant, place it in a shallow well of a dapping block with the letters facing down and tap lightly with the dap.

6 Open the jump ring with chain-nose pliers, insert it into the hole you've made, close the jump ring, and your pendant is ready to hang on a chain **(FIGURE 2)**.

MAKE IT YOUR OWN

- The photographs on pages 32 and 38 show creative variations of this project.
- Dangle a few circles of different sizes, attaching them with jump rings.
- String different shapes together.
- As your metalsmithing skills expand, try soldering a small shape onto a larger stamped shape.

TELL IT LIKE IT IS!

I love to stamp words that mean something to me and tell the world how I feel and what I believe in. If you're looking for ideas, here are some of my favorite words.

HAPPINESS	TRUST	GRACE
JOY	HUG	HONOR
BLISS	ENJOY	PASSION
CHEER	GRIT	DIGNITY
LAUGH	LIVE	GRIN
SING	HUMOR	LOVE
DANCE	ENDURE	CHERISH
PEACE	PREVAIL	INDULGE
SMILE	SURVIVE	FLY
GIGGLE	FLOURISH	FRIENDSHIP
SILLY	PROSPER	BOOGIE
BREATHE	SAVOR	CREATE
	THRIVE	

ID-STYLE BRACELET

Combine chain and flat wire for a quick, ID-style bracelet that is as unique as the wearer. Go retro by wearing your name (or your sweetheart's name) on your bracelet, use an inspirational word, or choose a short phrase that tells the world something about you!

TECHNIQUES

HOLE PUNCHING P. 24

OXIDIZING & POLISHING P. 30

STAMPING P. 36

MATERIALS

2" (5 cm) piece of 7 mm x 1 mm flat wire

6" to 8" (15 cm to 20.5 cm) of heavy chain (enough for bracelet to fit wrist loosely when attached to flat wire and clasp)

4 jump rings, 18-gauge, 4mm inner diameter

Toggle clasp

TOOLS

Letter/number stamp set and/or design stamps

Bench block

Safety glasses

Stamping hammer

Oxidizing solution

Pro Polish polishing pads or #0000 steel wool and polishing cloth

Permanent marker

Screw-down hole punch or drill and drill bits

Heavy cutters

File

Bracelet-bending pliers

Measuring tape

Chain-nose pliers

A second pair of chain-nose or flat-nose pliers to aid in opening and closing jump rings

FINISHED SIZE

$7^1/_2$" long x $^1/_4$" wide (19 cm x 6 mm)

TIPS & TRICKS

- **Shorten the length of the flat wire if you are making a bracelet for a small wrist or if your words are short and you don't want too much blank space. Don't use wire longer than 2" (5 cm), though—it won't flow and sit properly on the wrist.**

ID-STYLE BRACELET

1 Center your word and/or designs on the flat wire segment on the bench block, following the instructions on page 37. Put on your safety glasses, and stamp using a stamping hammer **(FIGURE 1)**.

2 Oxidize and polish the stamped wire.

3 Mark two dots on the stamped flat wire for the holes that will attach to the chain. Punch the holes with the screw-down hole punch or drill and drill bits **(FIGURE 2)**.

4 To round the edges of the wire, use heavy cutters to cut a tiny bit off of the corners of the wire; this will save you time in filing **(FIGURE 3)**.

5 File the edges to round them off **(FIGURE 4)**.

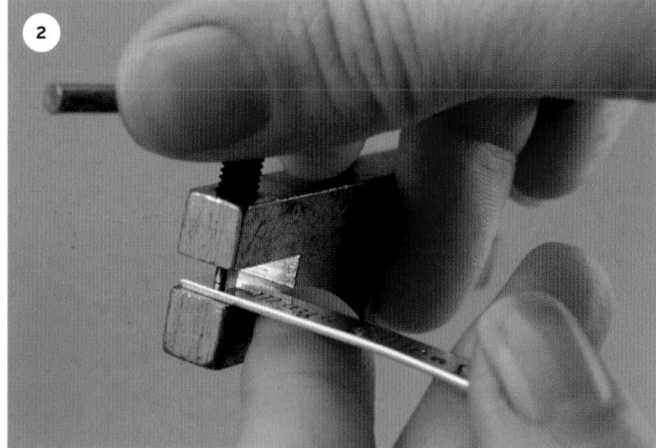

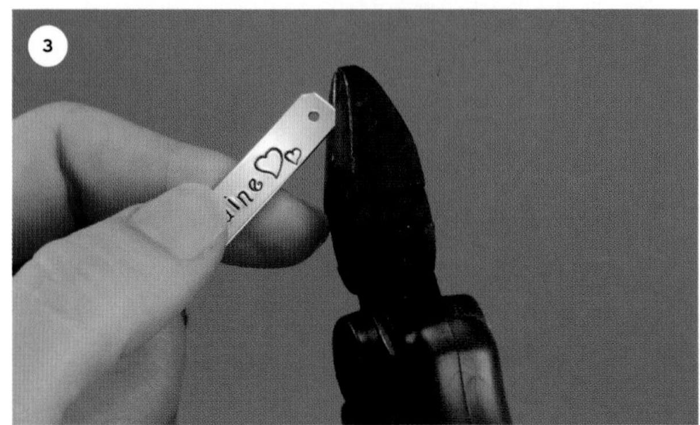

6 Using the bracelet-bending pliers, start at one end of the flat wire and squeeze the metal between the jaws of the pliers. Open the jaws, move the pliers down the metal about ½" (1.3 cm), and repeat **(FIGURE 5)**. Repeat for the full length of the flat wire **(FIGURE 6)**.

7 Measure the chain. Using the heavy cutters, cut two equal pieces (each will be attached to the flat wire on one end and a section of the clasp on the other end). The chain should add enough length so that the bracelet, when clasped, fits loosely around your wrist.

8 Open the jump rings with the chain-nose pliers (see page 132). Use two of the jump rings to attach the chain pieces to the flat wire. Use the remaining two jump rings to attach the ends of the chain to the two sections of the clasp **(FIGURE 7)**.

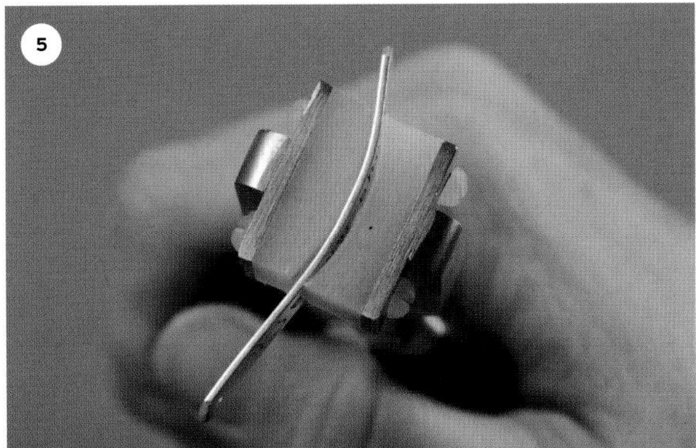

5

6

7

MAKE IT YOUR OWN

- Instead of attaching the chain to the plaque with jump rings, attach it with a wire-wrapped link with a bead to add color.
- String some beads together with beading wire and attach the plaque and the clasp with crimp beads.

STAMPED PREFABRICATED RINGS

Although you will learn techniques in this book to fabricate your own rings, stamping on premade rings will save you time and money. Prefabricated rings are available in various widths and sizes.

TECHNIQUES

OXIDIZING & POLISHING P. 30
STAMPING P. 36

MATERIALS

Prefabricated sterling silver ring in size and width desired

TOOLS

Tapered steel ring mandrel

Table vice with plastic or rubber clamp covers

Safety glasses

Letter/number stamp set and/or design stamps

Stamping hammer

Oxidizing solution

Pro Polish polishing pads or #0000 steel wool and polishing

FINISHED SIZE

Finished size varies according to the size of the prefabricated rings used.

TIPS & TRICKS

- The key to achieving clear, strong stamping on a ring is to have the clamp closed very tightly. The clamped ring mandrel should not move or wiggle at all. If you can move the ring mandrel, the ring will bounce when stamped, leaving a weak or shadowed impression.
- Due to the extreme curve of rings, there is little horizontal space on which to stamp each letter. This requires you to use fairly small letters and designs. I would suggest letters no larger than 3/32" (2.5 mm). To stamp a long design, tilt the stamp to one side, strike it, then tilt it to the other side and strike it. This technique is a bit risky because if you move your hand at all between the tilts and strikes, you won't get a clear impression.

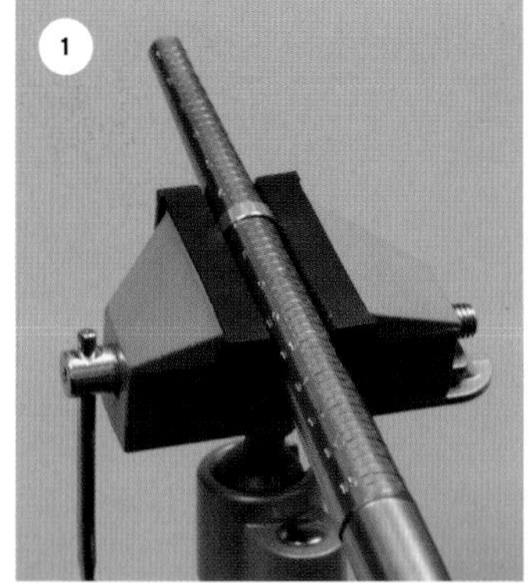

STAMPED PREFABRICATED RINGS

1 Slide your ring onto the mandrel until it sits snugly.

2 Open the clamp on the table vise. Insert the ring mandrel with the ring on it and tighten the clamp firmly **(FIGURE 1)**.

3 Put on your safety glasses. Stamp onto the exposed section of the ring **(FIGURE 2)**.

4 To stamp all the way around the ring, loosen the grip on the clamp and rotate the ring. Be sure to retighten the clamp between rotations.

5 Oxidize and polish the ring.

MAKE IT YOUR OWN

- Say it on your finger! Anything goes, as long as it'll fit on a ring.
- Stamp just one word at the top of the ring or stamp all around the ring.
- Make rings in sets to be worn together, with related words.

STAMP IN MANY LANGUAGES

Rings have been engraved or etched since the ancient Egyptians put hieroglyphics on jewelry. Today, rings are the perfect place for a romantic sentiment. As you search for ideas, don't overlook using words in other languages. It's a way to honor friends who are far away or to add meaning to a special phrase. Here are some popular words and phrases in foreign languages that require only a basic 26-letter alphabet stamp set. Look online or in foreign language phrase books for other translations.

I LOVE YOU

DANISH: Jeg elsker dig

FRENCH: j'taime

GERMAN: Ich liebe dich

ITALIAN: Ti amo

PORTUGUESE: Eu te amo

SPANISH: Te amo

BEAUTIFUL

DUTCH: Prachtig

FRENCH: Magnifique

ITALIAN: Bello

PORTUGUESE: Lindo

SPANISH: Bello

I MISS YOU

DANISH: Jeg savner dig

FRENCH: Tu me manques

GERMAN: Ich vermisse dich

ITALIAN: Mi manchi

SPANISH: Te echo de menos

PEACE

FRENCH: Paix

GERMAN: Frieden

ITALIAN: Pace

FOREVER

DANISH: Altid

FRENCH: Toujours

ITALIAN: Per sempre

SPANISH: Para siempre

SWEDISH: Evighet

FRIENDSHIP

GERMAN: Freundschaft

ITALIAN: Amicizia

SPANISH: Amistad

LINKED-SHAPES BRACELET

Animate shaped sterling silver blanks with stamping and link them together into a dynamic bracelet. Dress it up by linking similar shapes or express your whimsical nature by grouping a mix of shapes and beads.

TECHNIQUES

HOLE PUNCHING P. 24
OXIDIZING & POLISHING P. 30
STAMPING P. 36

MATERIALS

7 sterling silver blanks in various shapes and sizes (as shown, blanks are 12 mm to 25 mm in width)

7 sterling silver 7x5mm 16-gauge oval jump rings (or substitute 5mm inner diameter round jump rings)

14 sterling silver 3mm daisy spacers

12 bicone crystal 4mm beads

12 sterling silver 2" (5 cm) balled head pins

A few additional bicone crystal beads and/or daisy spacers for dangles (optional)

Sterling silver toggle clasp

3" (7.5 cm) of sterling silver 22-gauge dead soft wire

TOOLS

Permanent marker

Safety glasses

Screw-down hole punch, hole-punch pliers, or drill and drill bits

Letter/number stamp set and/or design stamps

Bench block

Stamping hammer

Oxidizing solution

Pro Polish polishing pads or #0000 steel wool and polishing cloth

Bracelet-bending pliers

Chain-nose pliers

A second pair of chain-nose or flat-nose pliers to aid in opening and closing jump rings

Round-nose pliers

Flush cutters

Plastic or rawhide mallet (optional)

FINISHED SIZE

Bracelet shown is about $7\frac{1}{2}$" x 1" (19 cm x 2.5 cm)

TIPS & TRICKS

- **If stamping distorts the metal blanks, use a plastic or rawhide mallet to flatten them on a bench block.**

LINKED-SHAPES BRACELET

1 On each of the blanks, mark holes on both sides, so the blanks can be linked together with jump rings.

2 In the center blank (in this case, the round washer shape), mark two additional holes on the top and bottom to add bead dangles.

3 Center your words and/or designs on the blanks, following the instructions on page 37, and stamp using a stamping hammer **(FIGURES 1A AND 1B)**.

4 Put on your safety glasses. Punch or drill holes at the markings.

5 Oxidize and polish the blanks.

6 Give each blank a slight curve by squeezing them with bracelet-bending pliers **(FIGURE 2)**.

7 Using chain-nose pliers, open the jump rings (see page 132) and link the stamped blanks together **(FIGURE 3)**.

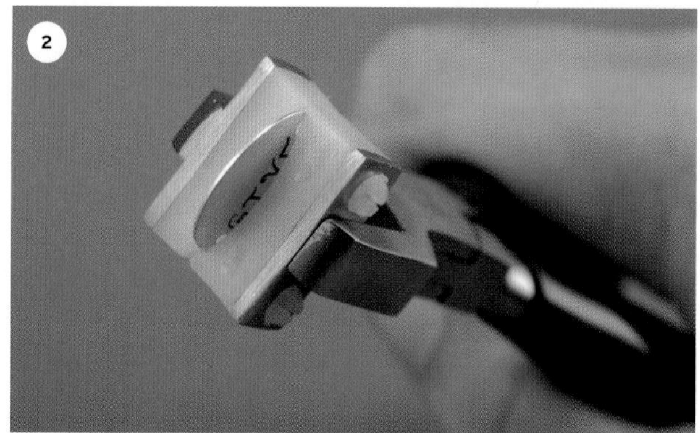

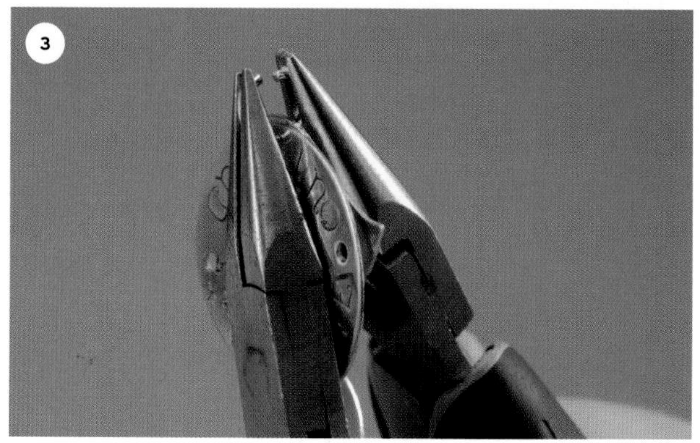

8 String one spacer and one bicone crystal onto each of ten head pins. Use round-nose pliers to form a wrapped loop to create a dangle (see page 133). Make ten dangles. If desired, use additional crystal bicones and/or spacers to vary some of the dangles with up to two beads and two spacers, as shown in **FIGURE 4**.

9 Using a jump ring, link the loop side of the toggle clasp to one side of the bracelet.

10 Link the T-bar section of the clasp to the other end of the bracelet. Use the 22-gauge wire to form a wrapped loop that attaches to one side of the bracelet. String on a spacer bead, six wrapped loop dangles, and one spacer. Form a second wrapped loop that attaches to the T-bar. Trim any excess wire with flush cutters.

11 To embellish the center blank, use a head pin and string one spacer and one bicone. Form a wrapped loop that attaches to one side of the blank. Add two of the dangles made in Step 8 into that loop before wrapping it closed. Repeat on the other side of the center blank to complete the bracelet **(FIGURE 5)**.

MAKE IT YOUR OWN

- Add wire-wrapped dangles to all the stamped shapes to add more movement and texture to this bracelet.

SAY IT ON YOUR WRIST

To properly size this cuff bracelet, measure the exact circumference of your wrist at the place where you wish the cuff to sit. Subtract ½" (1.3 cm) from that measurement; the result is the correct length to cut your metal. These instructions are for the "princess" bracelet shown.

TECHNIQUES

OXIDIZING & POLISHING P. 30
STAMPING P. 36

MATERIALS

Sterling silver flat wire, 5 mm or 6 mm wide and at least 1 mm thick, or a strip cut and filed from sheet metal at least 18-gauge

TOOLS

Measuring tape

Safety glasses

Heavy cutters

Letter/number stamp set and/or design stamps

Bench block

Stamping hammer

Oxidizing solution

Pro Polish polishing pads or #0000 steel wool and polishing cloth

Nail buffer, sanding sticks, or sandpaper

Heavy file

Bracelet bending pliers, or steel oval bracelet mandrel and plastic or rawhide mallet

FINISHED SIZE

Bracelets shown are about 6" x 1/4" (15 cm x 6 mm).

TIPS & TRICKS

- Be careful stamping any single vertical letters such as *i* or *l*. Those lines will thin and weaken the metal in such a way that it may bend at those spots. When shaping the bracelet, support these spots in the jaw of your pliers, or with your fingers, to avoid any sharp bends.
- Be sure to write out the words that you plan to stamp on this bracelet and follow the instructions on page 37 to center them.

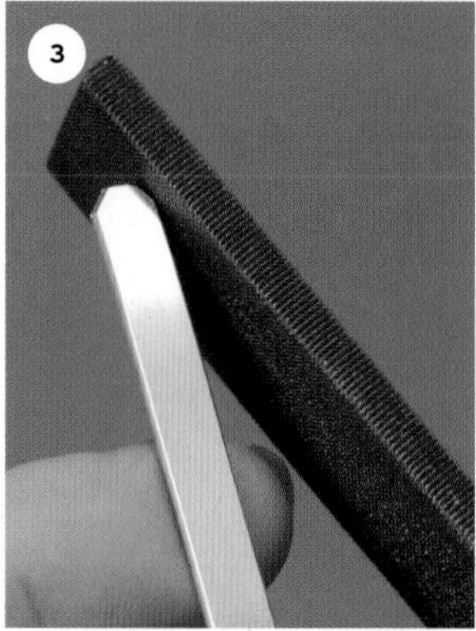

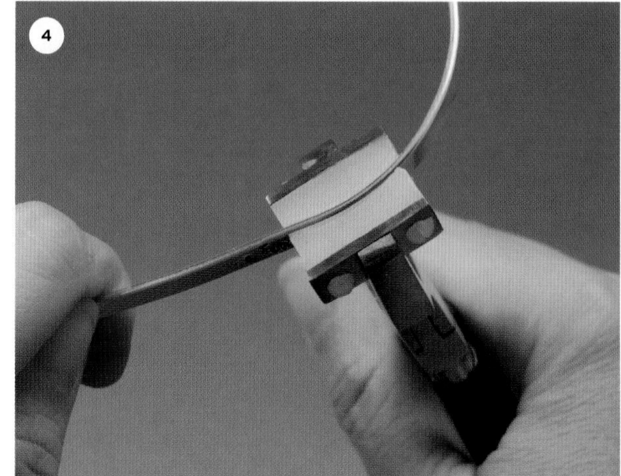

SAY IT ON YOUR WRIST

1 Measure your wrist as described on page 54. Put on your safety glasses and use heavy cutters to cut the metal to the desired size.

2 Write out the words you plan to stamp. If there are multiple words, note the amount of letters and spaces. Determine the center of the word or phrase, put on your safety glasses, and begin stamping the metal on the bench block from that center point. Align the designs with the letters on the metal and stamp **(FIGURE 1)**.

3 Oxidize and polish your stamped words and designs. Before filing the edges, trim the end corners with heavy cutters—this makes for less filing **(FIGURE 2)**.

4 Using a heavy file, file and round the outside ends **(FIGURE 3)**. When the shape is complete, switch to a nail buffer, sanding sticks, or sandpaper to create a final smooth polish.

5 Using the bracelet-bending pliers, start at one end of the metal and squeeze the metal firmly between the jaws of the pliers. Open the jaws of

the pliers, scoot the metal down 1/4" (6 mm), and squeeze. Continue to do this until you have worked on the whole length of the metal **(FIGURE 4)**. The metal should now be in an open "C" shape.

6 Using the bracelet-bending pliers as a handle, hold the outer 1/2" (1.3 cm) of the metal, bracing the remaining metal in the cupped palm of your hand. Begin to lightly bend the outer section of the metal **(FIGURE 5)**. Be deliberate about where you work this bend. The parts of the metal in your hand and in the pliers will not move. Bend the metal into more of an oval shape, to better fit the wrist.

7 Optional: You can also bend the metal on a steel oval bracelet mandrel, if available, using a plastic or rawhide mallet to hammer the metal into shape on the mandrel. Annealing the metal will allow it to properly shape around the mandrel (see page 31).

8 Your bracelet is now complete **(FIGURE 6)**. Put it on and say it on your wrist!

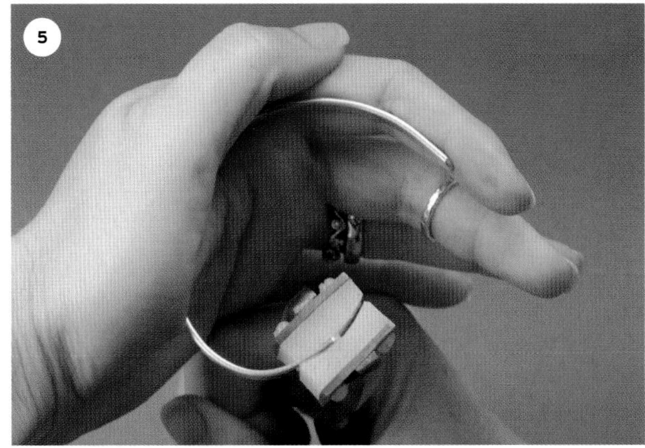
5

6

MAKE IT YOUR OWN

- Tube-rivet a stamped copper blank to the center of a sterling silver cuff (see page 28). Rivet the blank on before bending the bracelet.
- Drill holes in each end of the cuff and attach a decorative clasp with 5mm inner diameter jump rings.

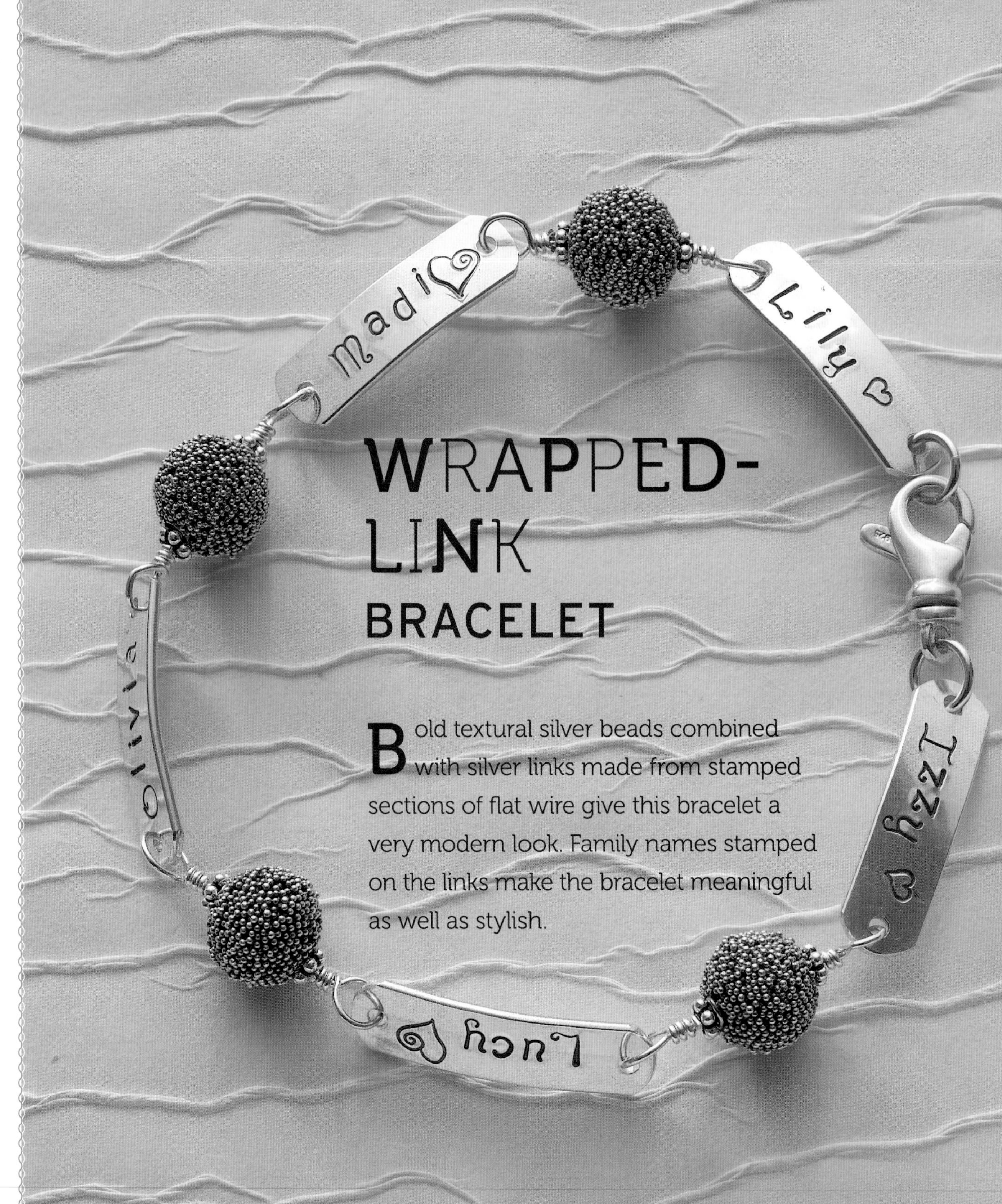

WRAPPED-LINK BRACELET

Bold textural silver beads combined with silver links made from stamped sections of flat wire give this bracelet a very modern look. Family names stamped on the links make the bracelet meaningful as well as stylish.

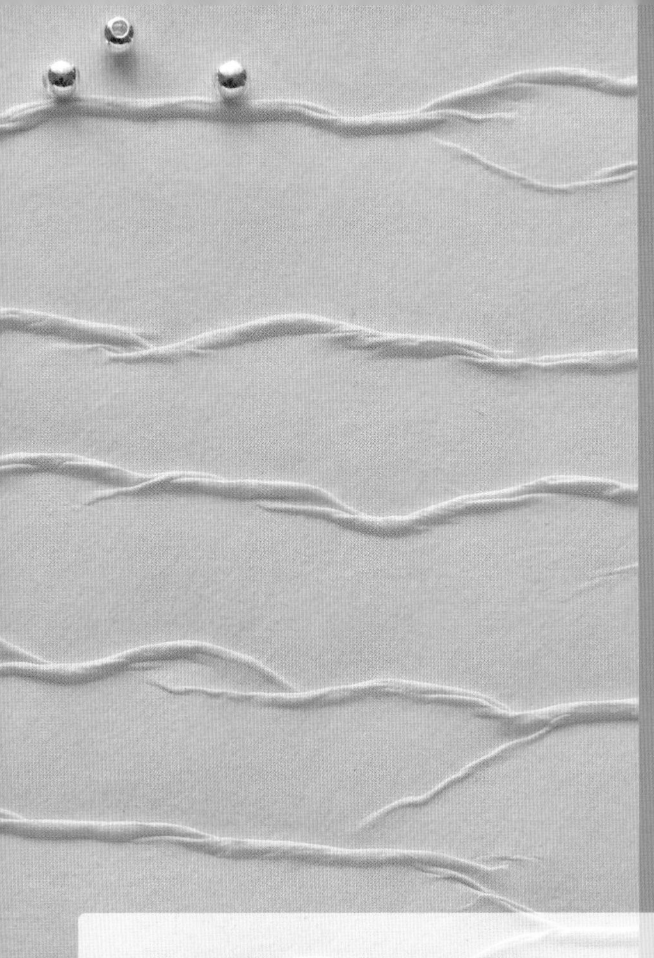

TECHNIQUES

CUTTING & SAWING P. 23
HOLE PUNCHING P. 24
OXIDIZING & POLISHING P. 30
STAMPING P. 36

MATERIALS

- 6" (15 cm) of sterling silver flat wire, 7 mm wide x 1 mm thick
- 15" (38 cm) of sterling silver 22-gauge dead-soft round wire
- 8 silver 4mm spacer beads
- 4 beads, 10mm
- Jump ring, 16-gauge, 6mm inner diameter
- Jump ring, 16-gauge, 4mm inner diameter
- Sterling silver lobster clasp, 13mm

TOOLS

- Safety glasses
- Heavy cutters, with capacity to cut the 7x1 mm wire
- Permanent marker
- Screw-down hole punch or drill and drill bits
- Heavy file
- Bench block
- Letter/number stamp set and/or design stamps
- Stamping hammer
- Oxidizing solution
- Pro Polish polishing pads or #0000 steel wool and polishing cloth
- Bracelet-bending pliers
- Round-nose pliers
- Chain-nose pliers
- A second pair of chain-nose or flat-nose pliers to aid in opening and closing jump rings
- Flush cutters

FINISHED SIZE

Bracelet shown is $8^3/_4$" (22 cm) long

TIPS & TRICKS

- The sizing on this bracelet is a bit tricky. I chose to make all my links the same size, but you can also size them according to word length. I cut each link to 7/8" (2.2 cm), knowing that I wanted five links and my four wrapped-loop links would measure about 3/4" (2 cm) each. (I made a test bracelet in copper to work out the math.) Add the length of the clasp.

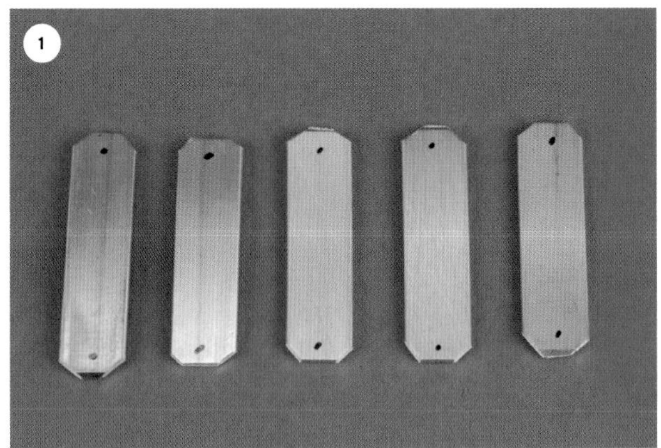

WRAPPED-LINK BRACELET

1 Choose the words and designs for each link and write them down.

2 Put on your safety glasses. With heavy cutters, cut your flat wire to the desired lengths. In the bracelet shown, the links are 7/8" (2.2 cm).

3 Trim off the corners of each link with the heavy cutters (this makes for less filing later). Using a permanent marker, mark spots for holes on each end of each link, about 2 mm in from the edge of the wire. You'll make wire-wrapped loops through these holes to connect each bead unit **(FIGURE 1)**.

4 Using the smaller side of the screw-down hole punch, make a hole at each mark on the links.

5 Using a heavy file, file the ends of each link into a rounded shape.

6 Stamp the links on a bench block, following the instructions on page 37 for centering words and designs. Oxidize and polish all links **(FIGURE 2)**.

7 Squeeze each link with bracelet-bending pliers to give them a slight curve. This will make the bracelet lie comfortably on your wrist.

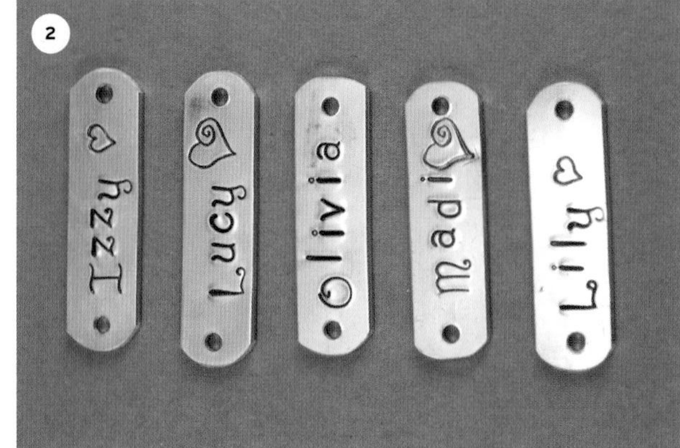

8 Wire-wrap the links together (see page 133). Begin with a 3" (7.5 cm) piece of 22-gauge wire. Use the round-nose pliers to make a loop on one side, stringing the stamped blank onto that loop before wrapping it closed. String on a Bali silver spacer bead, a 10mm decorative bead, and another Bali spacer bead. Make a loop on the other side of the wire, connecting it to the next stamped blank before wrapping it closed.

9 Open the jump rings with two pairs of chain-nose pliers (see page 132). Attach the lobster clasp to an ending link with the smaller jump ring. Attach the larger jump ring through the open hole in the other ending link **(FIGURE 3)**.

MAKE IT YOUR OWN

- Wire-wrap prefabricated blanks together or cut pieces from sheet metal (make sure it's at least 20-gauge).
- Use matching "statement" beads or make every bead different.

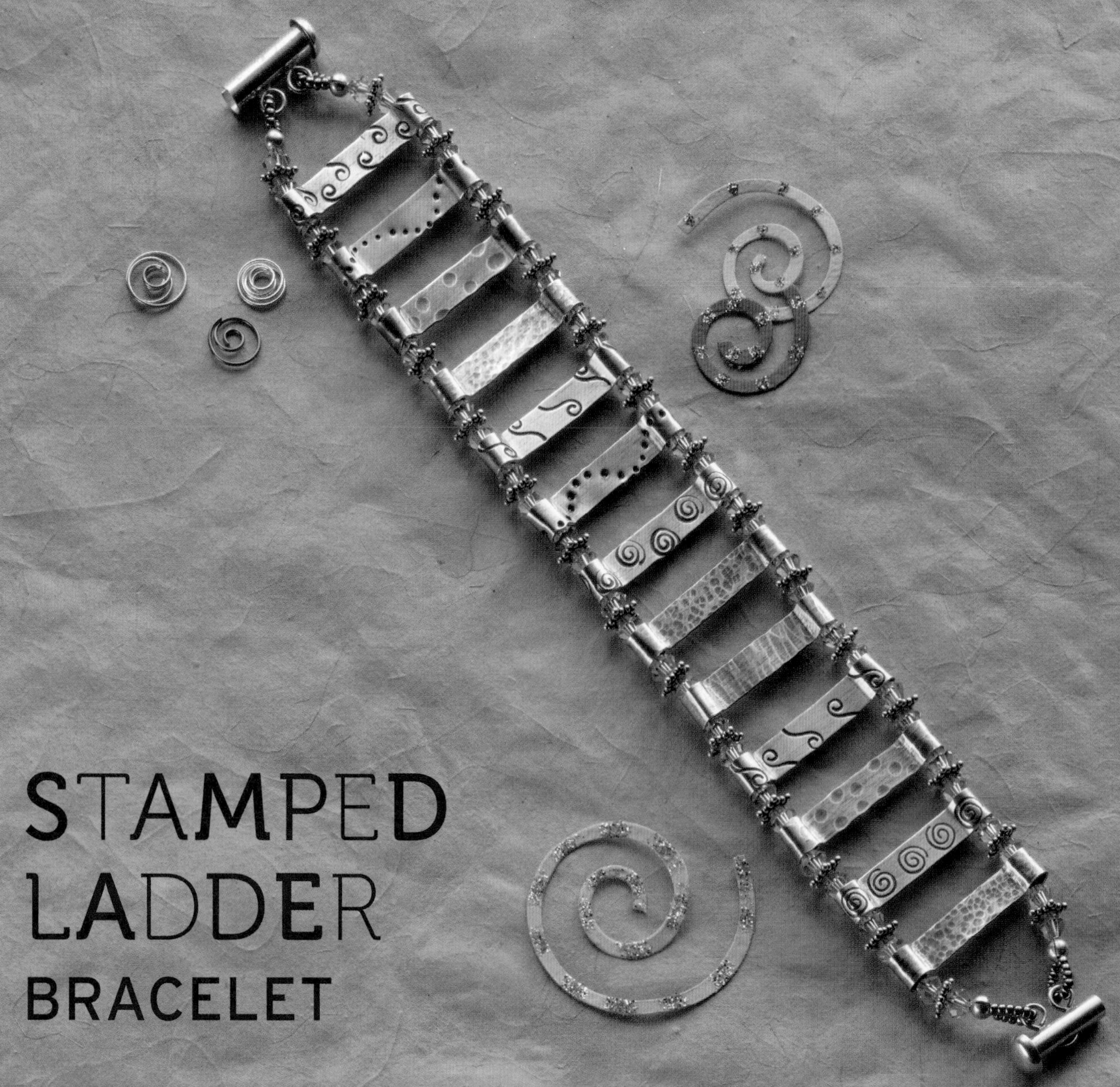

STAMPED LADDER BRACELET

In this project, it's essential to use stepped round-nose pliers. Standard round-nose pliers won't properly turn in the edges of the strips because of the taper of the jaw. I chose 4mm bicone crystals because I like the way the tapered ends of the beads fit into the loops of the stamped strips, stabilizing them.

TECHNIQUES

HAMMERING & TEXTURING P. 22

OXIDIZING & POLISHING P. 30

STAMPING P. 36

MATERIALS

27" (68.5 cm) of sterling silver 26-gauge bezel wire (to make up to 15 strips)

Copper sheet metal for practice

24" (61 cm) of beading wire

68 Swarovski crystal 4mm bicone beads

38 star-shaped 4mm or 5mm Bali silver spacers

4 crimp tubes

40 size 15° seed beads to cover beading wire where the bracelet joins the clasp

1 two-strand tube slider clasp

4 crimp tube covers

TOOLS

Safety glasses

Flush cutters

Permanent marker

Letter/number stamp set and/or design stamps

Bench block

Stamping hammer

Oxidizing solution

Pro Polish polishing pads or #0000 steel wool and polishing cloth

Stepped round-nose pliers with a 2 mm to 3 mm step

Chain-nose pliers

Tape

Crimping pliers

FINISHED SIZE

Bracelet shown is 7" (18 cm)

NOTE: A 7" (18 cm) bracelet requires 13 stamped metal strips. For a larger bracelet, each additional unit of stamped strip plus bicone, spacer, bicone will add about 7/16" (1.2 cm).

TIPS & TRICKS

- Remember, 26-gauge wire is very thin metal. When stamping letters, don't stamp as hard as you usually would. Be very careful with letters that have a long vertical line (such as a lowercase *i* or *l*) because they'll thin out the metal further, and the metal will want to bend and possibly break at that spot.
- Sometimes a metal strip will curve if letters are stamped too close to either the top or the bottom (long edges) of the metal strip. To keep your strip straight and even, try to center the letters between the top and bottom of the strip as much as possible. If your design goes to the edge, balance the amount of stamping on the top and bottom. It's okay to stamp all the way to the short edges.

STAMPED LADDER BRACELET

1 Put on your safety glasses. Using flush cutters, cut the bezel wire into 1¾" (4.5 cm) strips.

2 Decide on words and/or designs for the strips. In the bracelet shown, I textured all the pieces using various hammers and design stamps. Practice stamping and texturing techniques on copper sheet metal first before stamping on the sterling silver strips. The strips in **FIGURE 1** were textured as shown, from left to right:

- **a** ball-peen end of a chasing hammer, tapped with medium force
- **b** ball-peen end of a chasing hammer, hit very hard to get a more solid dot (that placement was a bit tricky)
- **c** spiral design stamp
- **d** period stamp or a center punch
- **e** rectangular end of a riveting hammer, tapped with medium force

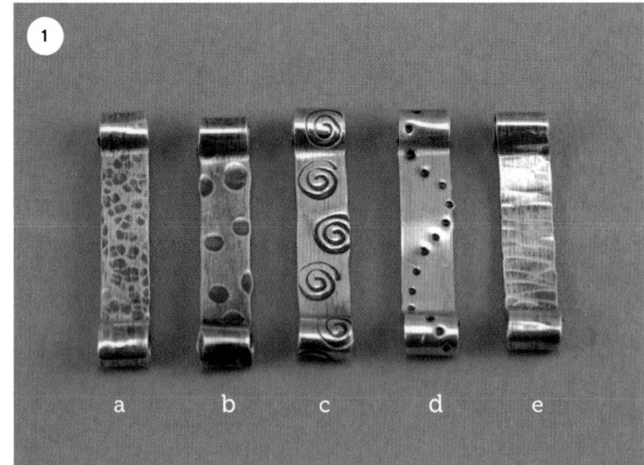

3 To stamp words on your strips, first write out each word to ensure correct spelling and count the number of letters. The initial length of each strip is 1¾" (4.5 cm). The rolled-in edges take up ½" (1.3 cm) on either end, leaving about ¾" (2 cm) of stampable area.

4 With a marker, make a mark ½" (1.3 cm) in from each end **(FIGURE 2)**. Center your word in the space between the marks, as described on page 37, and stamp.

5 Once all the pieces are stamped, oxidize and polish the strip before rolling in the ends.

6 Using the 2 mm to 3 mm step of the stepped round-nose pliers, grasp the end of the wire and turn a basic loop **(FIGURE 3)**.

7 Let the wire come around and then slightly overlap. Don't push on it too hard when it overlaps or you will get a teardrop shape. Let it lightly come around and overlap on top of itself **(FIGURE 4)**.

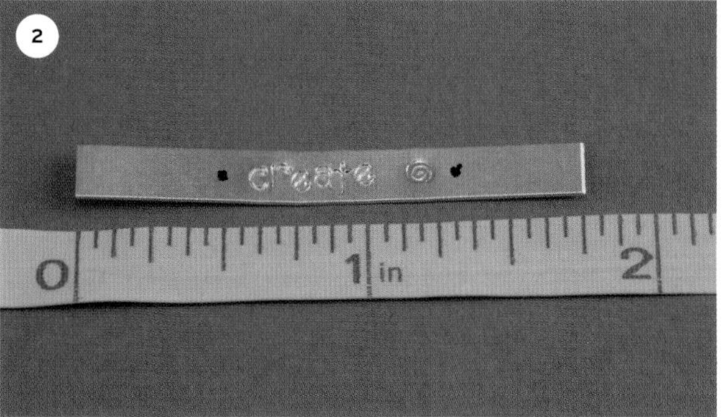

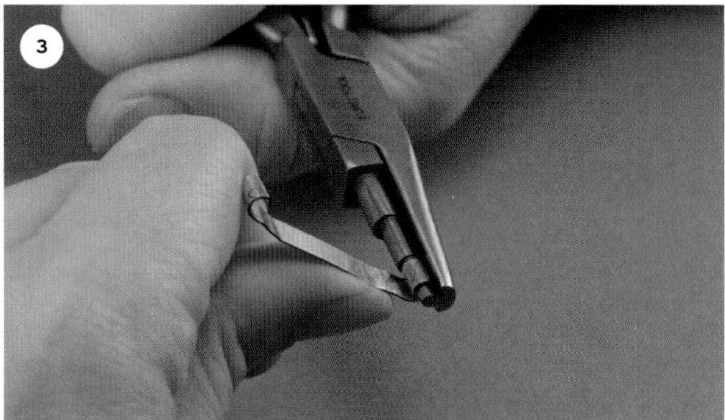

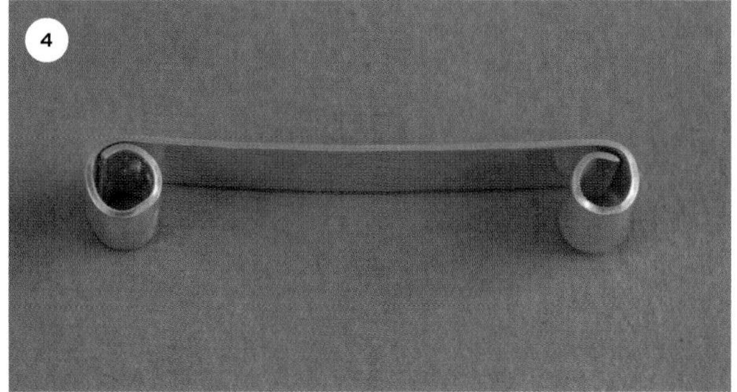

8 Use chain-nose pliers to grab the inside of the loop and position the inside edge (in this case, the left edge) of the pliers on the center of that loop, just above the overlap. **FIGURE 5** shows the correct placement of the pliers; **FIGURES 6 AND 7** show incorrect placement.

9 Hold the loop in the chain nose and kink it to center. Repeat on the other side. **FIGURE 8** shows a side view of the kinked strip, while **FIGURE 9** shows a top view.

10 Repeat for all the strips. Place the strips side by side and check to see that they are the same length. If you measured correctly and used the same step on the stepped round-nose pliers, the strips should all line up.

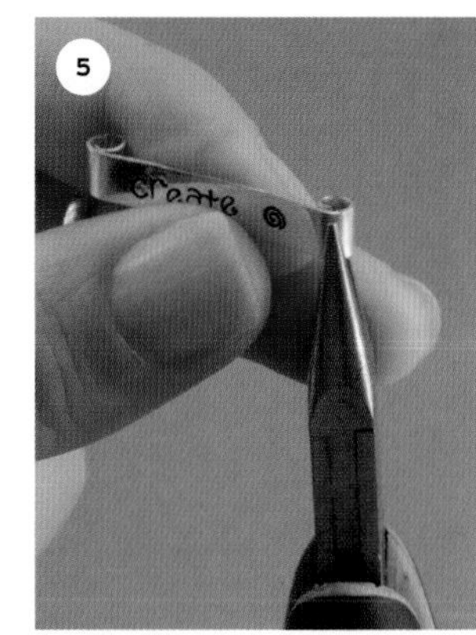

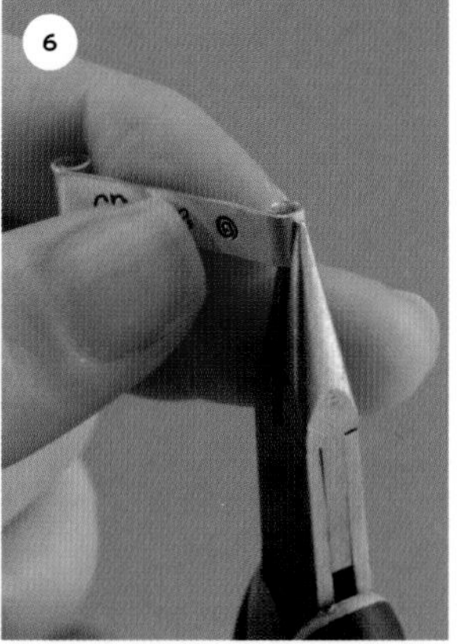

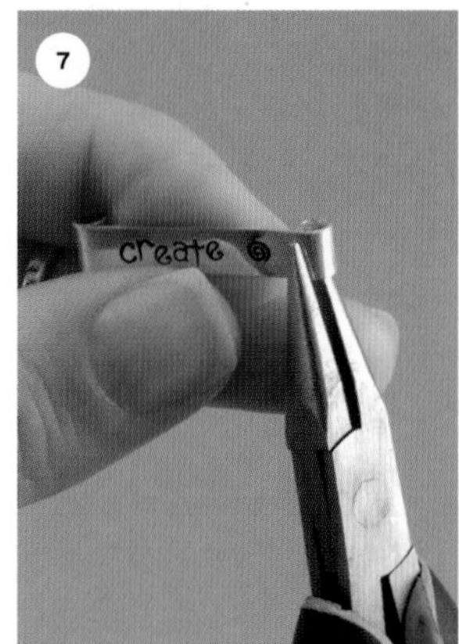

MAKE IT YOUR OWN

- Taper the ends of the ladder strips.
- Stamp words on the ladder strips to write out a favorite saying.

11 Cut two 12" (30.5 cm) pieces of beading wire. Fold a piece of tape around one end of each wire to prevent the beads from falling off while you're stringing. String beads and strips in the following order: bicone, Bali spacer, bicone, strip, repeat. String simultaneously on both top and bottom wires. After stringing all of the strips, finish each wire with a bicone, Bali spacer, bicone, crimp tube, and 10 seed beads **(FIGURE 10)**.

12 String each wire through a loop on the clasp and back through the crimp tube **(FIGURE 11)**. If the seed beads don't fit through the loop on the clasp, string on that clasp loop between the fifth and sixth seed bead. Crimp the crimp tubes closed (see page 132).

13 Trim the tail of each wire with the tip of the flush cutters and cover the crimp tubes with crimp tube covers **(FIGURE 12)**.

14 Slide the tape off the other end of each wire, add the crimp tubes and seed beads, and complete as you did on the first side.

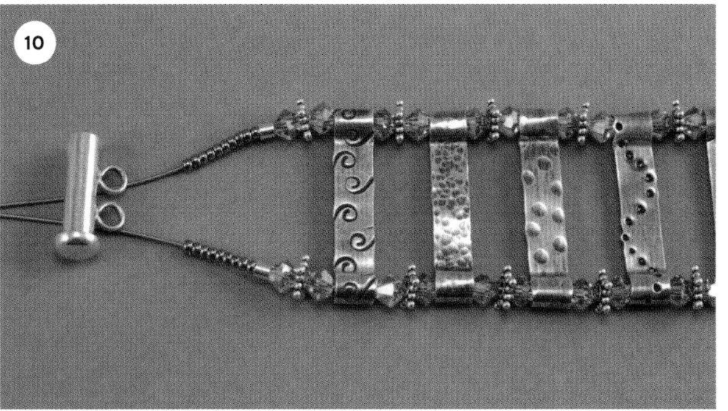

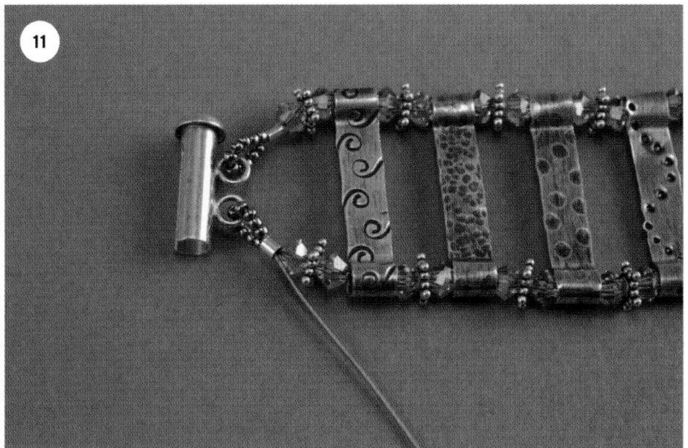

STAMPED & STACKED
RING

This project uses many of the metalsmithing techniques learned in this book. Adding a riveted blank on the top makes a truly unique ring. These instructions are for the ring shown with silver and copper flower shapes, stamped with a bird and sun.

TECHNIQUES

HOLE PUNCHING P. 24
DAPPING P. 26
RIVETING P. 27
OXIDIZING & POLISHING P. 30
ANNEALING P. 31
STAMPING P. 36

MATERIALS

½" (1.3 cm) of sterling silver 14-gauge round wire for rivet

1" (2.5 cm) of sterling silver flat wire, 5 mm wide x 1.5 mm thick

Sterling silver flower blank, ½" (1.3 cm) diameter

Copper flower blank, ⅝" (1.5 cm) diameter

TOOLS

Safety glasses

Table vise

Riveting hammer

Metal jeweler's ruler

Permanent marker

Heavy cutters

Heavy file

Butane torch for annealing

Cooling cup (a glass or metal cup or small bowl with cool water in it)

Chasing hammer

Drill and size #52 drill bit, or 1.8 mm hole-punch pliers

Bench block

Letter/number stamp set and/or design stamps

Stamping hammer

#0000 steel wool and polishing cloth

Metal dapping block

Oxidizing solution

Large Wrap 'n' Tap pliers (with barrel sizes 13 mm, 16 mm, and 20 mm)

Tapered steel ring mandrel

FINISHED SIZE

Finished size will vary according to ring size.

TIPS & TRICKS

- The holes you punch in the two ends of the flat wire and in the two dapped blanks must accommodate a 14-gauge riveting wire. If you've punched any holes that are too small, ream them out with a file or bead reamer tip.
- As you rivet the dapped blank to the top of the ring, be very careful. If the riveting hammer slips off the rivet during hammering, it will hit your dapped blank and mar it.

STAMPED & STACKED RING

1 Put on your safety glasses. Make a nailhead rivet on the 14-gauge wire, as shown on page 28.

2 Refer to the chart and ring sizing instructions on page 73 to determine how far apart to punch your holes for the size ring you wish to make. Measure and mark that distance on the flat wire. Using heavy cutters, cut the wire 4 mm beyond those dots on either side. Do not punch the holes yet.

3 To make the ring band, file the ends to a round shape, then anneal the metal, following the instructions on page 31. We'll flatten the ends of the metal in the next step; annealing makes it softer and easier to flatten. If the annealing process removes your hole marks, measure and mark them again.

4 Using a chasing hammer, flatten both ends **(FIGURE 1)**.

5 The metal ends will splay as you flatten them. Use a heavy file to file off the splayed edges of the metal **(FIGURES 2 AND 3)**.

1

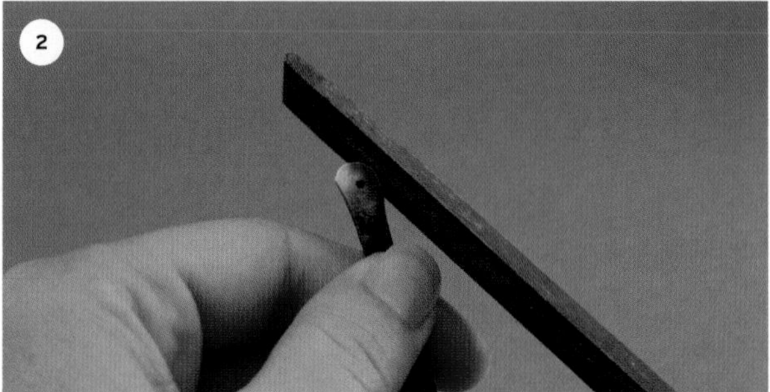
2

3

6 Drill or punch the holes on either end.

7 On the bench block, stamp your words and/or designs on the ring band and anneal the metal again **(FIGURE 4)**. This adds darkness to the inside of the stamped images and softens the band so you can properly shape it into a ring.

8 Buff the fire scale off of the surface with #0000 steel wool.

9 Prepare the two blanks to be riveted onto the ring by first punching a hole in each one, then stamping, lightly dapping, oxidizing, and polishing. Note that there is no stamping on the lower (copper) blank, because only its edges will show **(FIGURE 5)**.

10 Shape the band into a round ring shape. I use large Wrap 'n' Tap pliers to assist in shaping. Hold the very end of the metal with the tool on the second step and roll it in halfway **(FIGURE 6)**.

4

5

6

11 Flip to the other side of the metal and repeat **(FIGURE 7)**.

12 Place the band on the steel ring mandrel and continue to shape it. Bring the ends of the metal wire around until they overlap and the holes line up.

13 Slide the band off of the mandrel, keeping the ends overlapped. Insert the nailhead rivet (made in Step 1 from 14-gauge wire) from the inside of the ring through the holes in the overlapped ends **(FIGURE 8)**.

14 Stack the two dapped blanks onto the 14-gauge wire, convex side up. Slide the whole ring back onto the ring mandrel and trim the riveting wire to extend 1.5 mm above the top blank **(FIGURE 9)**.

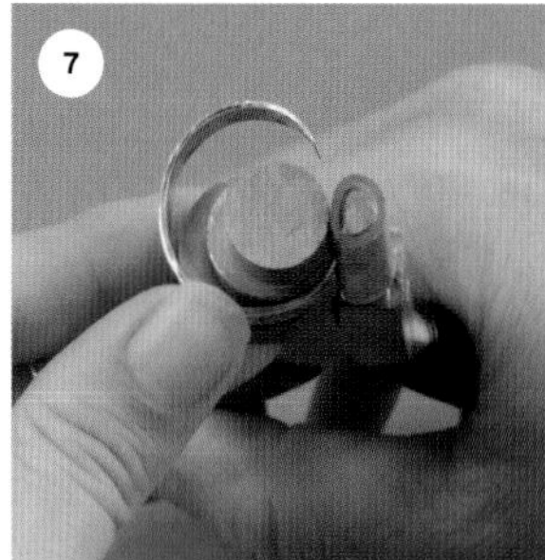

7

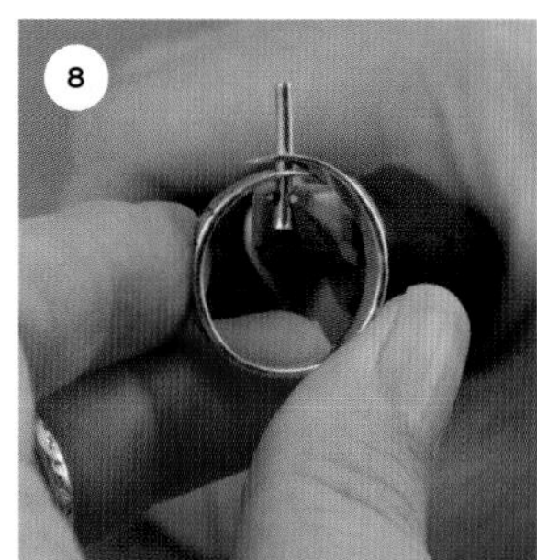

8

9

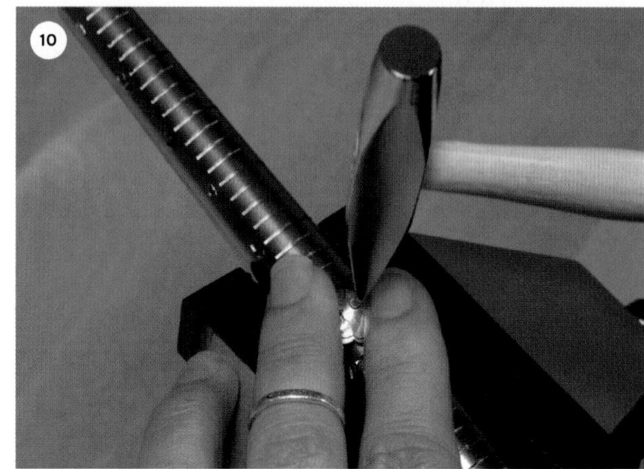

10

MAKE IT YOUR OWN

- The star ring shown combines two blanks—a circle and a star—with a dot stamped on each point of the star, then uses a central rivet to connect the two blanks and the ring base. The words Rock Star are stamped on the band.
- The heart ring shown has a hammered-metal heart blank with a tiny heart punched out of one corner. The word Always is stamped on the band.

15 Clamp the ring and ring mandrel tightly in a table vise with plastic or rubber clamp covers.

16 As you prepare to finish the rivet, notice how I hold the ring in **FIGURE 10**. I intentionally protect most of the flower blanks with my fingers so I don't accidentally slip off the rivet and mark the blank. Rivet the wire down to complete the ring **(FIGURE 11)**.

Ring Sizing

To properly size a ring, you must consider the size of the desired ring, its inner diameter, the thickness of the metal, and, in this case, the fact that the ends of the metal overlap. The chart below shows the inner diameter and the corresponding ring size.

Using the chart, determine the inside diameter for the size ring you wish to make.

Add to that number the thickness of the wire you're using to make the ring.

Multiply that number by pi, or 3.14. This is the length of metal needed to make that size ring. For the Stamped & Stacked Ring project, add 2 mm to account for the height of the overlap. For this project, this formula will determine the distance between the two riveting holes. Do not cut to this measurement; just mark and punch the holes at this length.

FORMULA Inner diameter + thickness of metal × 3.14 = X + 2 mm = distance between the two riveting holes. Add 8 mm to this for the total length of cut wire.

EXAMPLE To make a size 7 ring using wire that is 1.5 mm thick: 17.35 mm + 1.5 mm = 18.85 mm × 3.14 = 59.18 mm + 2 mm = 61.18 mm between the two riveting holes. Add 4 mm to each side (a total of 8 mm) for a total wire length of 69.18 mm.

U.S. RING SIZE	INSIDE DIAMETER IN INCHES	INSIDE DIAMETER IN MILLIMETERS
4	.585"	14.86 mm
5	.618"	15.70 mm
6	.650"	16.51 mm
7	.683"	17.35 mm
8	.716"	18.19 mm
9	.748"	18.99 mm
10	.781"	19.84 mm
11	.814"	20.68 mm
12	.846"	21.41 mm

TEXTURED-METAL PENDANT

This project appeals to sculptural wire fans who like very few rules. Cut a shape from sheet metal, stamp, texture, and then finish with a bead-and-wire-embellished edge and a riveted focal center. I used spiral design stamps of different sizes to texture the metal.

TECHNIQUES

CUTTING & SAWING P. 23
HOLE PUNCHING P. 24
RIVETING P. 27
OXIDIZING & POLISHING P. 30
STAMPING P. 36

MATERIALS

1" x 3" (2.5 cm x 7.5 cm) piece of 24-gauge sterling silver sheet metal

Blank disc, about ½" (3.8 cm) diameter (I used a sterling silver flower disc)

Flat 10mm Bali silver bead with a 14-gauge hole

½" (1.3 cm) of sterling silver 14-gauge round wire, to form the center rivet

6' (183 cm) of 24-gauge sterling silver dead-soft round wire

25 bicone crystals, 3mm to 4mm, in chosen color palette

18 Bali silver beads, no larger than 4.5mm

TOOLS

Pendant template

Paper

Scissors

Permanent fine-tip marker

Metal scribe (optional)

Safety glasses

Metal shears

Bench block

Design stamps

Stamping hammer

Metal jeweler's ruler

Center punch

Hole-punch pliers or drill and drill bits

Oxidizing solution

Pro Polish polishing pads or #0000 steel wool and polishing cloth

Flush cutters

Riveting hammer

Chain-nose pliers

Round-nose or stepped round-nose pliers

FINISHED SIZE

Pendant shown is 1⅜" wide x 2½" high (3.5 cm x 6.5 cm)

TIPS & TRICKS

- Use beads sparingly; fill space with wire.
- As you lace the embellishing wire through the holes in the pendant, go through each hole only once.
- Keep the wirework on the top front and the edge of the sheet metal; the wire hides the edge and the holes.

TEXTURED METAL PENDANT

1 Enlarge template on a copy machine to 200 percent. Cut out the paper template and trace it onto your sheet metal using a permanent marker or a metal scribe **(FIGURE 1)**.

2 Put on your safety glasses. Using metal shears, cut the shape out of the sheet metal **(FIGURE 2)**.

3 On the bench block, texture the shape with design stamps. Cover the entire metal shape except the top extension, which will become the bail of the pendant.

4 With a permanent marker, mark spots along the edges of the pendant (except the bail) for holes about ½" (1.3 cm) apart. These do not need to be exact, because they'll be covered with wirework and won't be visible. Carefully measure and mark a hole in the center of the metal shape **(FIGURE 3)**.

5 If using a drill to make holes, first use a center punch to mark each dot. This provides a dent to keep the drill bit in position. You can also use a pair of hole-punch pliers to punch the holes.

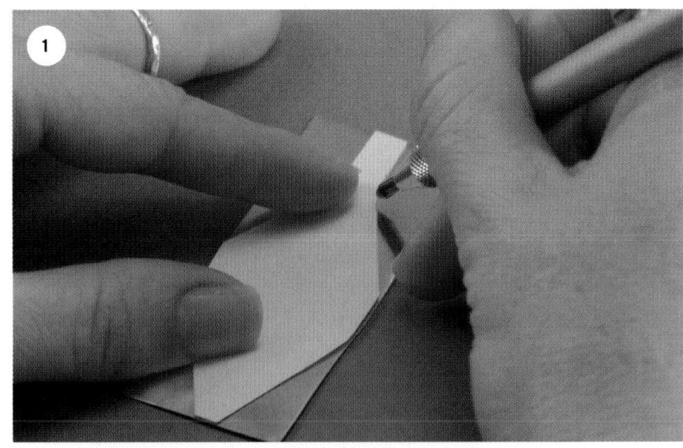

1

2

3

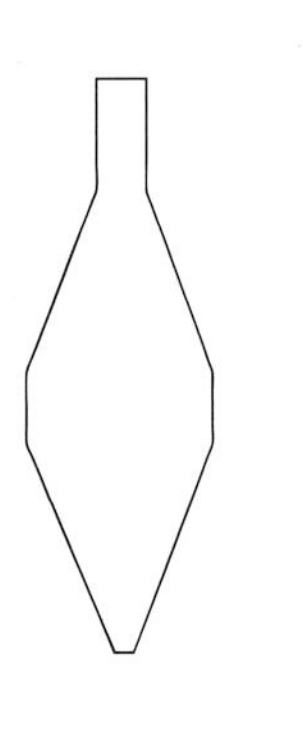

6 Drill the holes along the edges of the pendant first **(FIGURE 4)**. These holes must be big enough to accommodate a 24-gauge wire but should be no bigger than a 14-gauge hole.

7 Now drill or punch the center hole. This will be riveted using 14-gauge wire, so the hole must be exactly 14-gauge.

8 Carefully drill a hole in the center of the ½" (1.3 cm) blank disc. This, too, should be exactly 14-gauge in size.

9 Oxidize and polish the pendant. At the same time, roll the length of 24-gauge wire into a small coil and oxidize it, too.

10 Layer the pendant, the blank disc, and the Bali silver flat bead on top, aligning the 14-gauge holes. Insert the 14-gauge wire. Mark the wire on either end about 1 mm beyond the holes and cut the wire with flush cutters. Rivet the wire with the riveting hammer **(FIGURE 5)**.

11 To add the sculptural wirework, begin with a 3' (91.5 cm) section of 24-gauge wire.

12 Starting at any hole on the edge, pull the wire through halfway. Work with just one half of the wire first.

13 Loop the wire loosely through four holes, adding a bead or two on the loops **(FIGURE 6)**.

4

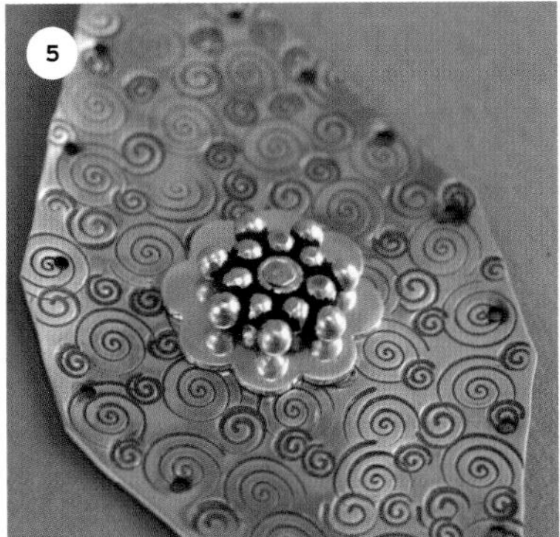
5

6

14 Now backtrack and loop your wire up, around, and through the existing loops, but going through each hole in the pendant itself only once **(FIGURE 7)**. Keep this random and unstructured. You can add beads as you go, but do so sparingly.

15 Using the tip of a pair of chain-nose pliers, grab any overly loose wires and rotate the pliers a half turn. This tightens the wire and provides a nice bit of texture **(FIGURE 8)**.

16 Continue working around the outer edge of the pendant in this manner until there is about 1" (2.5 cm) of wire remaining. Coil and wrap this last piece into a section of wire already involved in the edge work. Form two wraps. Use the chain-nose pliers to help tighten the wraps. Trim the tail with flush cutters.

17 Wrap the second 3' (91.5 cm) section of 24-gauge wire in the same manner on the other side of the pendant, looping and adding beads until the entire rim of the pendant is covered.

18 Go around one more time with wire only, looping and tweaking it with chain-nose pliers. This adds one final layer of texture **(FIGURES 9 AND 10)**. Polish the surface of the wirework with a Pro Polish pad.

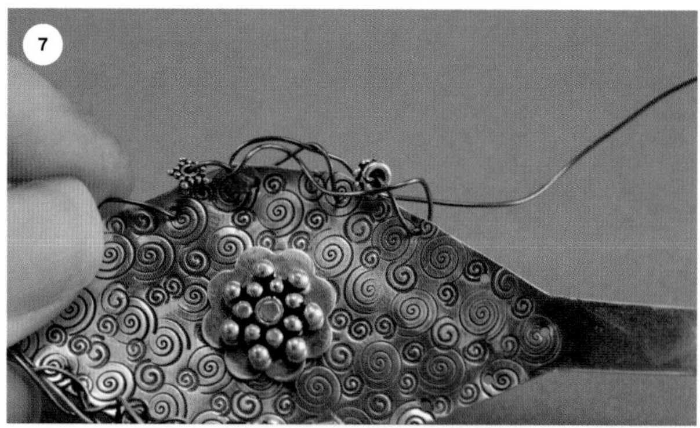
7

8

9

19 To complete the bail, use a 5 mm spot on your round-nose or stepped round-nose pliers and roll the top strip around and down to meet the back of the pendant **(FIGURE 11)**. Make sure it comes around tightly, butting securely against the back of the pendant **(FIGURE 12)**.

20 Hang the finished pendant on a chain or beaded strand.

10

MAKE IT YOUR OWN

- Use a limited bead palette or mix up colors, sizes, and finishes. There are infinite possibilities! The Bali silver beads can vary, too, for more texture and complexity.
- Make the pendant a different shape. Try a rectangle, a square, or an oval. Draw a template first and be sure to add an extension to make a bail.

11

12

LEATHER CUFF

In this project, I used a prefabricated rectangle blank with rounded corners. Feel free to change it up—use a different shape or cut your own custom shape from sheet metal. The contrast of supple leather and stamped metal makes a striking bracelet that you can wear with everything.

TECHNIQUES

HOLE PUNCHING P. 24

RIVETING P. 27

OXIDIZING & POLISHING P. 30

STAMPING, P. 36

MATERIALS

- Metal blank rectangle with rounded corners, 1 3/8" x 3/4" (3.5 cm x 1.8 cm)
- Leather strip, 7/16" (1.2 cm) wide, the measurement of your wrist plus 1" (2.5 cm)
- About 1" (2.5 cm) of thin-wall 2.5 mm sterling silver tubing
- Leather snap, 3/8" (1 cm)

TOOLS

- Safety glasses
- Bench block
- Letter/number stamp set and/or design stamps
- Stamping hammer
- Permanent marker
- Center punch
- Screw-down hole punch, hole-punch pliers, or drill and drill bits
- Oxidizing solution
- Pro Polish polishing pads or #0000 steel wool and polishing cloth
- Leather hole punch
- Tube-cutting pliers
- Jeweler's saw
- Bracelet-bending pliers
- Snap-setter set

FINISHED SIZE

Finished size will depend on the size of your wrist and the width of the stamped blank. The cuff shown is 7 1/2" (19 cm) long x 3/4" (2 cm) at its widest point.

TIPS & TRICKS

- **Use a precut leather strip, available at craft and hobby stores or leather shops, or cut your own from a large piece of leather.**

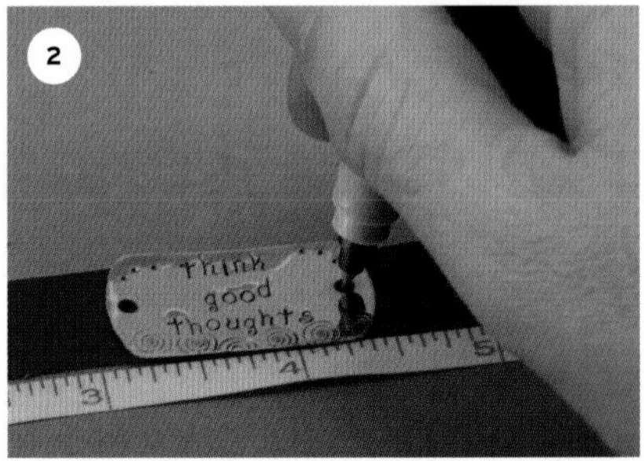

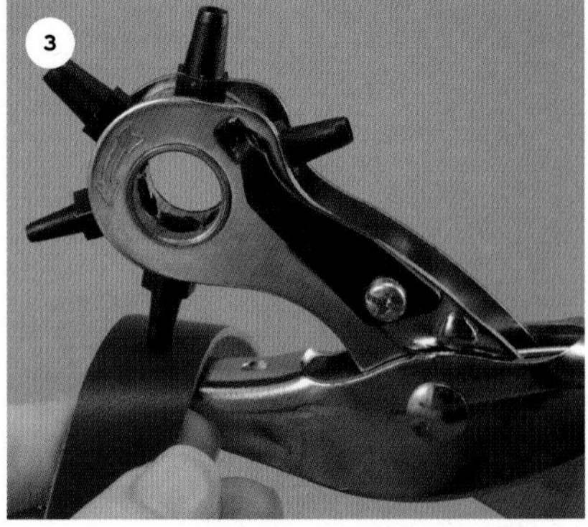

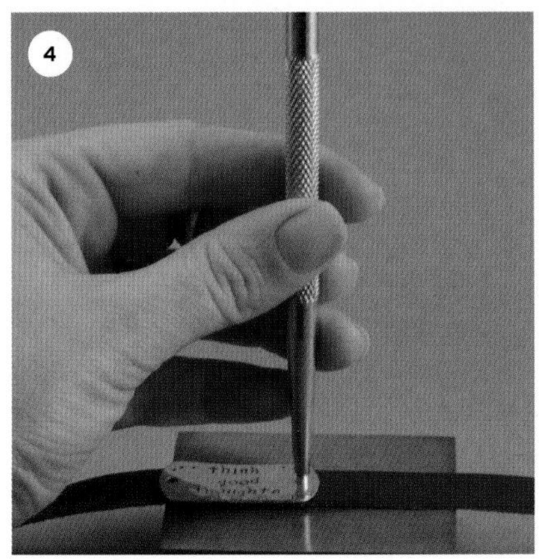

LEATHER CUFF

1 Put on your safety glasses. On the bench block, stamp your words/designs onto the metal blank. See page 37 for my method of centering the words and designs.

2 Mark and punch a hole centered on each short side of the metal blank, about 1/8" (2 mm) from the outer edge of the blank. Make sure the holes are large enough for the silver tubing to fit through.

3 Oxidize and polish the metal blank.

4 Center the stamped metal on the leather strip **(FIGURE 1)**.

5 Mark the location of the holes through the metal and onto the leather **(FIGURE 2)**.

6 Punch the holes in the leather using the leather punch. Use a punch size that is the same size or a bit smaller than the size of the sterling silver tubing **(FIGURE 3)**.

7 Insert the tube into the tube-cutting pliers and use the jeweler's saw to cut two appropriate lengths of tubing. Tube-rivet the metal to the leather **(FIGURES 4 THROUGH 8)**. See page 27 for complete riveting instructions.

8 Use bracelet-bending pliers to give the stamped blank a slight curve **(FIGURE 9)**.

9 Punch holes at each end of the leather strap for the closure snaps. Following the instructions for your snap setter, set snaps into the leather to complete the cuff.

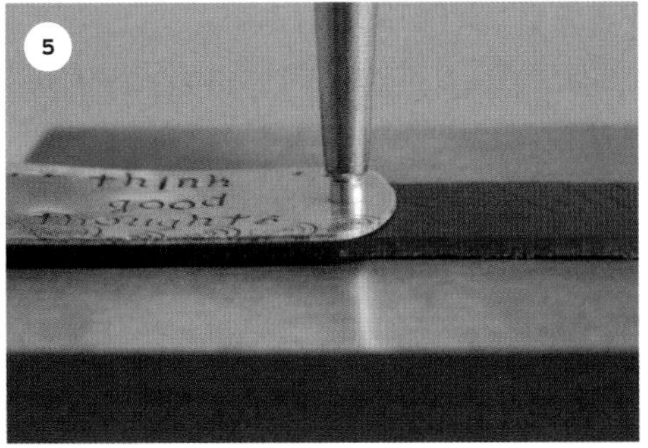

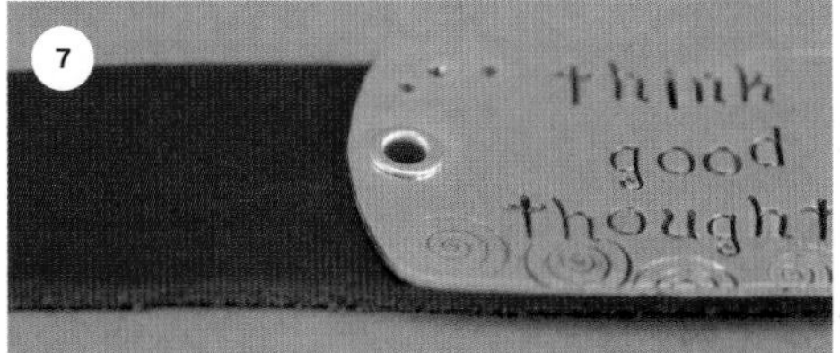

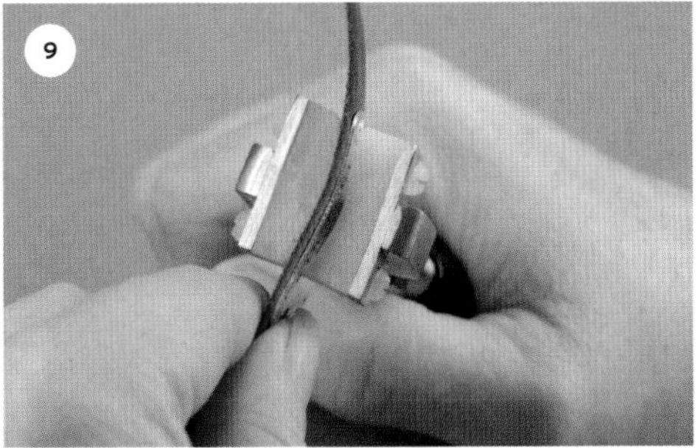

MAKE IT YOUR OWN

- Stitch seed beads or sequins on the leather strap to add more color and texture.
- Rivet an additional shape onto the plaque.

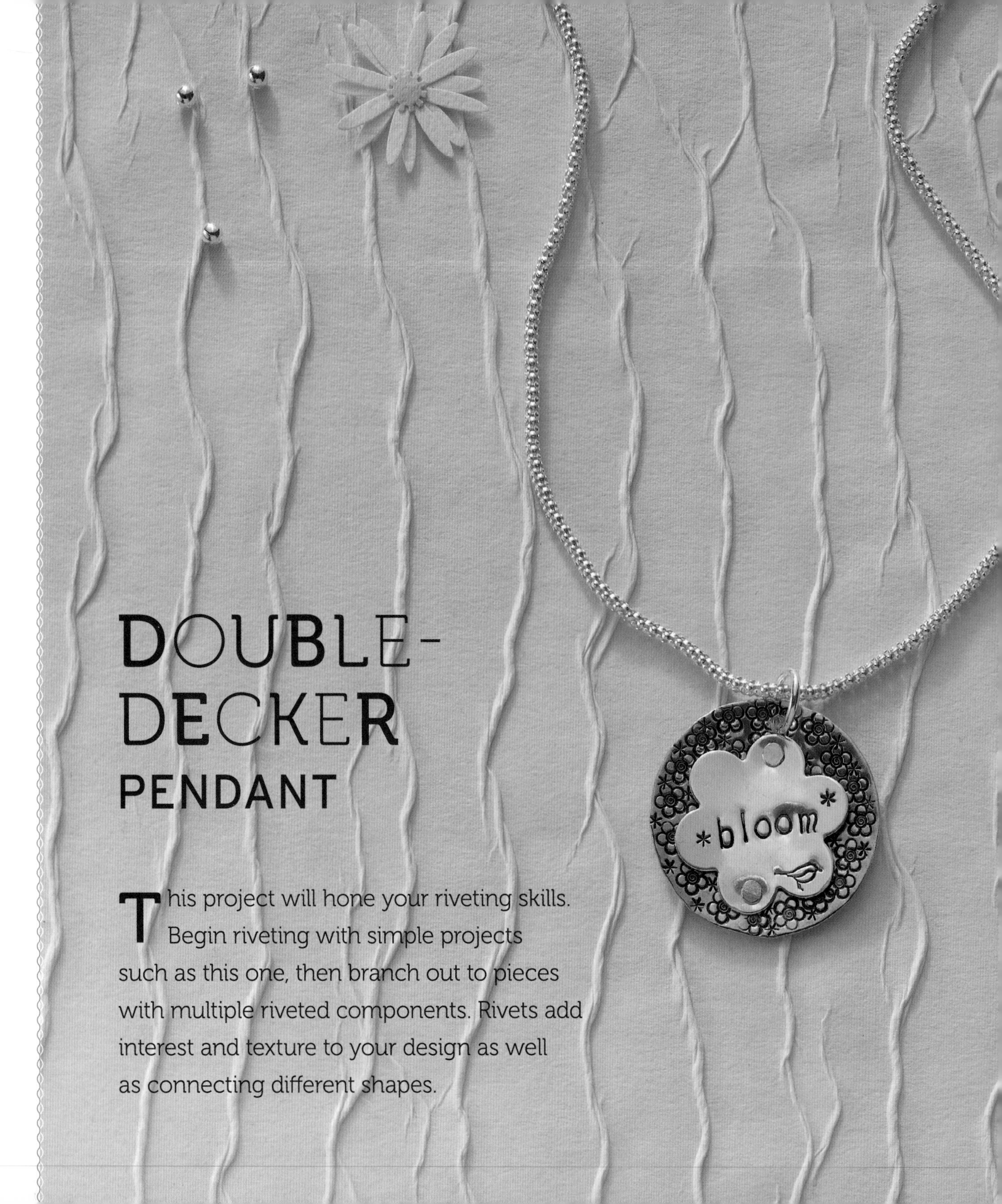

DOUBLE-DECKER PENDANT

This project will hone your riveting skills. Begin riveting with simple projects such as this one, then branch out to pieces with multiple riveted components. Rivets add interest and texture to your design as well as connecting different shapes.

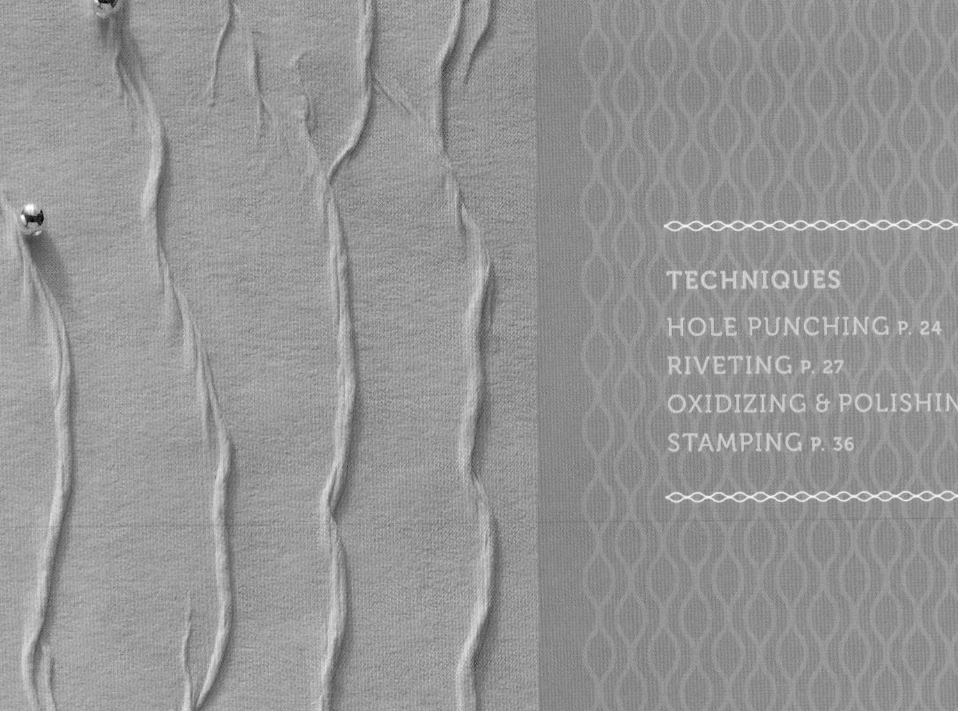

TECHNIQUES

HOLE PUNCHING P. 24
RIVETING P. 27
OXIDIZING & POLISHING P. 30
STAMPING P. 36

MATERIALS

2 prefabricated blanks in shapes of your choice

About 1" (2.5 cm) of sterling silver 14-gauge round wire, for two rivets

Jump ring, 18-gauge, 5mm inner diameter

TOOLS

Safety glasses

Bench block

Letter stamp set and/or design stamps

Stamping hammer

Chasing hammer

Oxidizing solution

Pro Polish polishing pads or #0000 steel wool and polishing cloth

Permanent marker

Hole-punch pliers

Flush cutters (capable of cutting 14-gauge wire)

File

Riveting hammer

Chain-nose pliers

A second pair of chain-nose or flat-nose pliers to aid in opening and closing jump ring

FINISHED SIZE

Pendant shown is about 1" (2.5 cm) in diameter. The finished size will be determined by the size of the larger of the two shapes used.

TIPS & TRICKS

- As you hammer down the first rivet, it sets both blanks into place. Make sure that the other hole or holes you've punched are properly lined up before tightly riveting that first one.

DOUBLE-DECKER PENDANT

1 Put on your safety glasses. On the bench block, stamp and/or texture both blanks with your desired design. Oxidize and polish the blanks before riveting **(FIGURE 1)**.

2 Mark and punch riveting holes in the top blank (pendant shown has two rivets).

3 Set the top blank over the bottom blank. Mark the bottom blank with the riveting holes through the holes in the top blank **(FIGURE 2)**.

4 Punch the riveting holes in the bottom blank.

5 Mark and punch another hole in the bottom blank for the jump ring.

6 Align the top and bottom blanks, matching the holes you've punched. Rivet them together through one of the holes. While riveting, make sure the remaining holes stay lined up. Be careful not to let the top blank shift.

7 Rivet through the second hole (and any additional holes that your design calls for).

8 Open the jump ring using two pairs of chain-nose pliers (see page 132). Insert the jump ring into the single additional hole in the bottom blank and close it to complete the piece **(FIGURE 3)**.

9 Add a chain to wear the pendant.

MAKE IT YOUR OWN

- Use design stamps to texture the larger blank and top it with a blank stamped with words.
- Use contrasting metals for an effective design; match the rivets to the metal of the larger blank.
- Cut your own shapes with metal shears instead of using prefabricated blanks.

DESIGNER * KRISS SILVA

SILVER-FRAMED GEMS PENDANT

Use fine silver bezel wire in an innovative way as you add a personal touch or stylistic element to a favorite statement bead. This technique also works well when added to the front of dapped blanks.

TECHNIQUES

HOLE PUNCHING P. 24
OXIDIZING & POLISHING P. 30
STAMPING P. 36

MATERIALS

Fine silver 26-gauge bezel wire, 3/16" (5 mm) wide, measuring the height of your bead plus 1/4" (6 mm)

1 balled 20-gauge head pin, long enough to go through the bead plus 1 1/2" (3.8 cm)

1 large flat bead (ours is about 7/8" wide x 1" high [2 cm x 2.5 cm])

1 sterling silver blank (ours is a 7/16" [11 mm] square blank with rounded corners)

2 sterling silver 16-gauge jump rings, 5mm inner diameter

TOOLS

Permanent marker

Safety glasses

Screw-down hole punch, hole-punch pliers, or drill and drill bits

Nylon-jaw pliers

Bench block

Letter/number stamp set and/or design stamps

Stamping hammer

Flush cutters

Medium-grit flat file

Round-nose pliers

Chain-nose pliers

A second pair of chain-nose pliers or flat-nose pliers to aid in opening and closing jump rings

Oxidizing solution

Pro Polish polishing pads or #0000 steel wool and polishing cloth

FINISHED SIZE

Pendant shown is 7/8" (2 cm) wide and 2" (5 cm) long

TIPS & TRICKS

- **This technique is an effective treatment for all your irregularly shaped stones and large beads.**

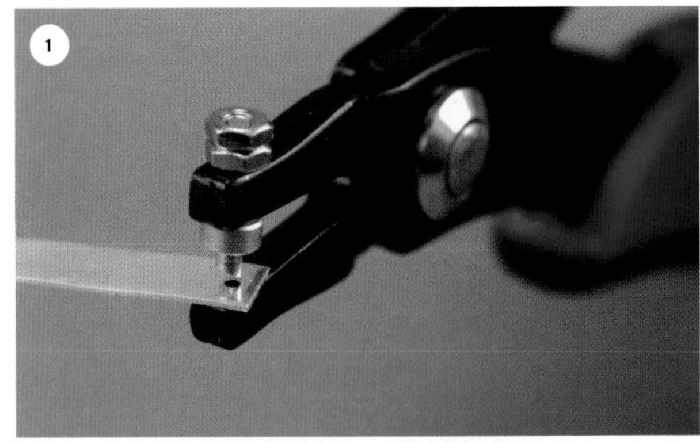

SILVER-FRAMED GEMS PENDANT

1 Using permanent marker, make a dot at one end of the bezel wire, about 2 mm from the edge of the wire. Put on your safety glasses and punch a hole for the 20-gauge head pin using a screw-down hole punch, hole-punch pliers, or a drill **(FIGURE 1)**.

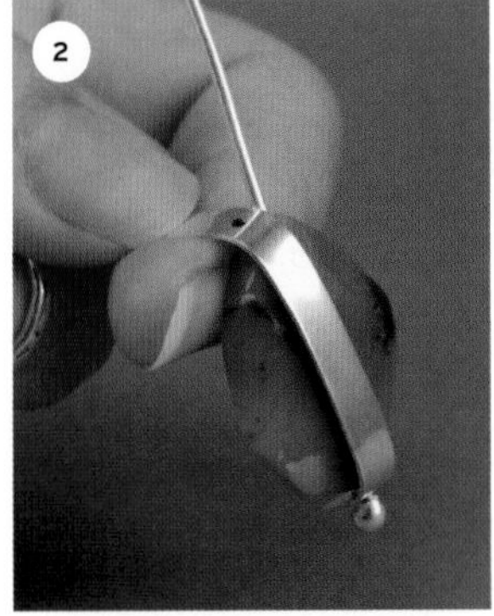

2 Thread the head pin through a hole in the bezel wire, then through the bead.

3 Pull the bezel wire and head pin firmly against the bead, up and then to the side of the head pin. Mark the metal to show where to punch your second hole. Make the mark slightly short (1 to 2 mm) to ensure a tight fit **(FIGURE 2)**.

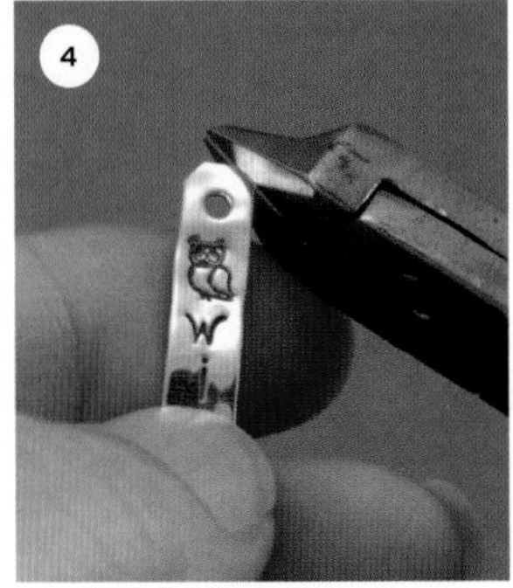

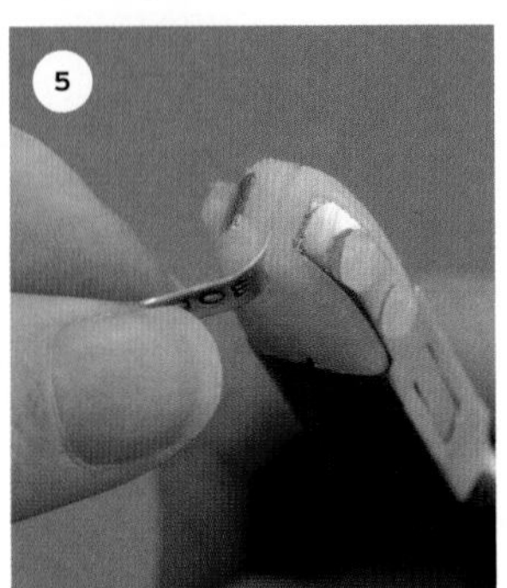

4 Take the wire and head pin off of the bead. Straighten the wire with the nylon-jaw pliers to prepare for stamping. Place the wire on the bench block and stamp your design, making sure it is not close to or beyond the marked dot. Punch the second hole on the wire where you marked the dot **(FIGURE 3)**.

5 With flush cutters, cut the corners off of both ends **(FIGURE 4)**. File the ends into a rounded shape.

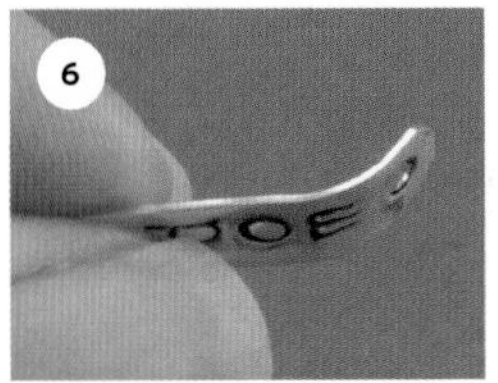

6 Using your nylon-jaw pliers, grab the end of the bezel wire up to the hole and a few millimeters beyond and give it a slight bend **(FIGURES 5 AND 6)**. Repeat on the other side **(FIGURE 7)**.

7 Insert your head pin through the bottom hole in the wire, through the bead, then through the top hole in the wire **(FIGURES 8 AND 9)**.

8 With round-nose pliers, form a wire-wrapped loop (see page 133) on the top of the bead **(FIGURE 10)**.

9 Stamp the square blank and punch holes in two corners.

10 Using two pairs of chain-nose pliers to open and close the jump rings (see page 132), connect the wire-wrapped loop at the top of the wrapped bead to the square blank with a jump ring. Connect one more jump ring to the top of the square to act as a bail.

11 Oxidize and polish your pendant.

12 Wear your pendant on a chain **(FIGURE 11)**.

8

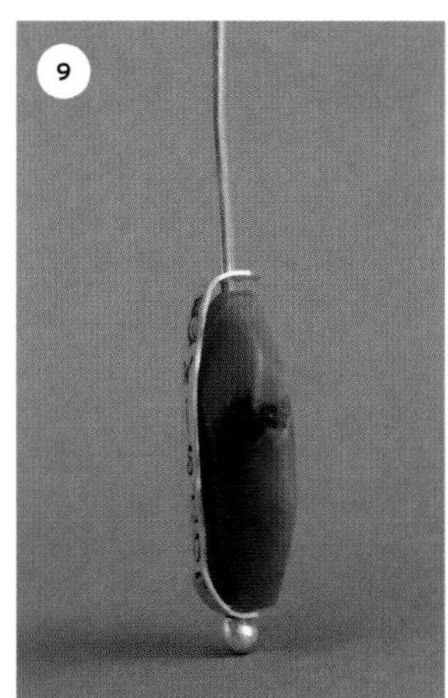
9

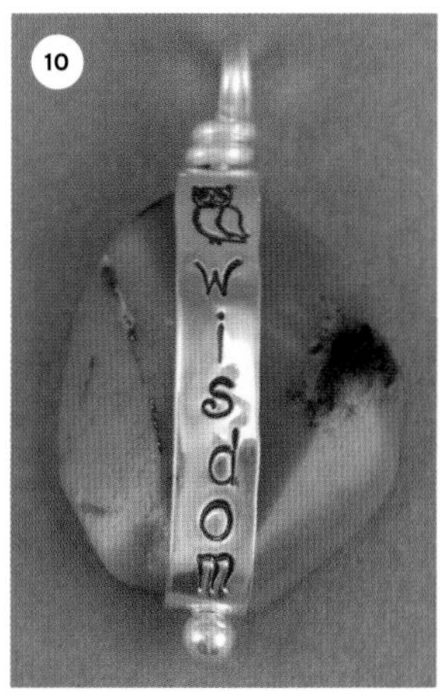

10

11

MAKE IT YOUR OWN

- Dangle beads or more stamped charms to add further detail to this design.

DESIGNER * JANICE BERKEBILE

THE CROWN JEWEL

Transform a large focal bead into a scrolled, dramatic pendant with stamping on the metal enclosure. Bead dangles add movement and further embellish the royal style of this pendant. Use a ball chain for your pendant to complete the bold look.

TECHNIQUES

CUTTING & SAWING P. 23
HOLE PUNCHING P. 24
OXIDIZING & POLISHING P. 30
STAMPING P. 36

MATERIALS

Sheet metal, 24 gauge, about 1" x 3" (2.5 cm x 7.5 cm)

5" (12.5 cm) of 14-gauge wire

3 thin cap-shaped beads, about 7mm to 8mm in diameter, with holes for 14-gauge wire

1 round or rondelle-shaped focal bead, about 25mm to 30mm, with a hole large enough for 14-gauge wire

3 or 4 large-holed components or beads with holes at least 7mm in diameter

4mm to 5mm bead or spacer with hole large enough for 14-gauge wire

2 large jump rings or chain links

Additional beads, spacers, and/or charms, for making dangles (optional)

TOOLS

Safety glasses

Metal shears

Medium-grit file

Hole-punch pliers (to punch 1.8 mm hole)

Bench block

Letter/number stamp set and/or design stamps

Stamping hammer

Oxidizing solution

Pro Polish polishing pads or #0000 steel wool and polishing cloth

Flush cutters

Chain-nose pliers

A second pair of chain-nose pliers or flat-nose pliers to aid in opening and closing jump rings

FINISHED SIZE

Pendant is about 3" long x 1" wide (7.5 cm x 2.5 cm)

TIPS & TRICKS

- Large-holed flat beads can be hard to find; try using copper washers dapped to conform to the bead's curvature (see page 26 for information on dapping).

THE CROWN JEWEL

1 Put on your safety glasses. Using metal shears, cut three strips of 24-gauge metal, each $^{1}/_{8}$" to $^{3}/_{16}$" wide by 3" long (3 mm to 4 mm wide by 7.5 cm long) **(FIGURE 1)**. The larger your focal bead, the wider the metal can be.

2 Round the corners of the strips using metal shears and a file.

3 Using the hole-punch pliers, punch a 1.8 mm hole in only one end of each of the three strips, about $^{1}/_{16}$" (2 mm) from the edge of the strip and centered.

4 Place a strip on the bench block. Using letter/number and/or design stamps and a stamping hammer, stamp each strip from the bottom hole about halfway up the strip **(FIGURE 2)**. Rotate the metal strips and turn them over. Now stamp the top half of the strips using the same designs **(FIGURE 3)**. If you are using a design stamp that has a "right reading," such as a martini glass, when you rotate the metal over, make sure you flip it upside down as well or your martini will spill!

5 Oxidize and polish the stamped metal strips.

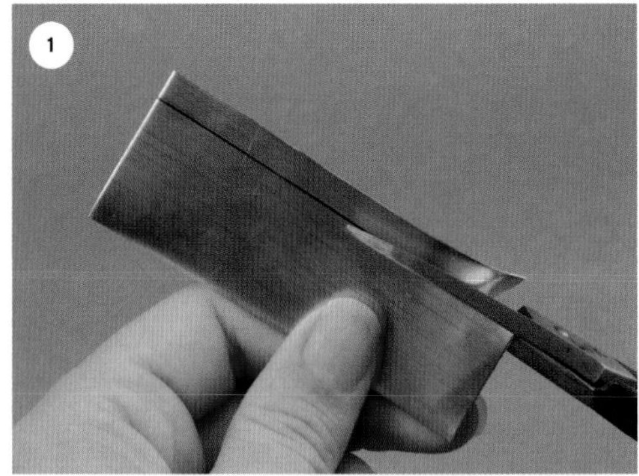

6 Make a spiral on one end of the 14-gauge wire (see page 133). Make two full rotations **(FIGURE 4)**. Make sure you leave space in the center of the spiral large enough for a large jump ring.

7 Plan the order for stringing the beads, spacers, and components **(FIGURE 5)**.

8 Insert the 14-gauge wire through two of the thin cap-shaped beads, then through the bottom holes in all three textured strips, with the texture closest to the holes facing outward. String the focal bead. Working on each strip separately, form the metal strips around the bead. Press the very end of the strips up against the bead with the back of chain-nose pliers.

9 Pinch the three metal strips together at the top of the bead.

10 String the large-holed beads (or dapped washers) over all three strips and the 14-gauge wire **(FIGURES 6 AND 7)**.

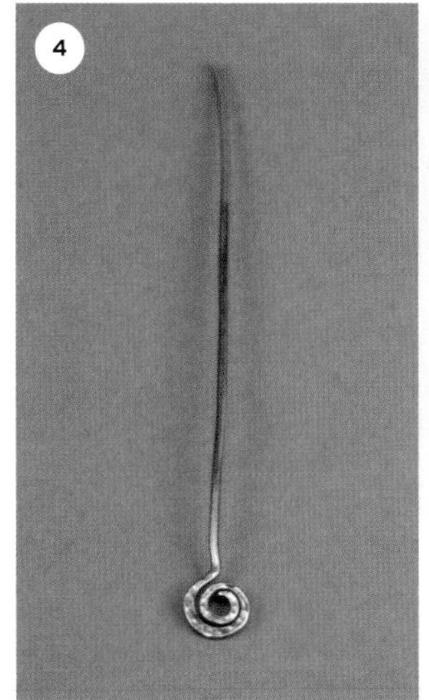
4

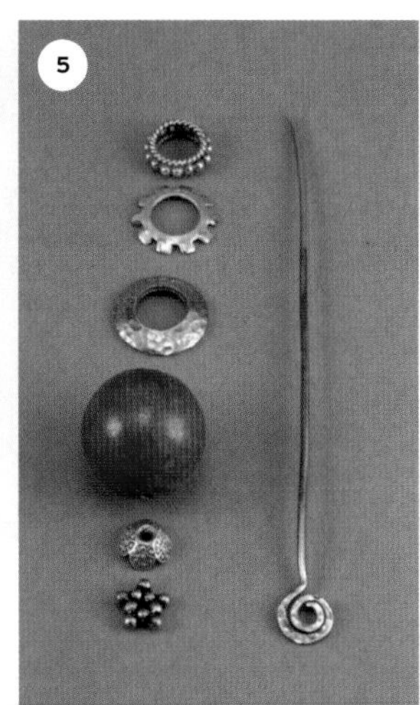
5

6

7

11 Scroll the strips of metal away from the wire, working on the tips of round-nose pliers **(FIGURES 8 AND 9)**.

12 Slide a very small bead or spacer that just fits over the wire to help maintain the balance. Then add a cap or a spacer to cover the three strips at the bottom.

13 Add a few more beads on the top, if desired.

8

9

14 With all components strung, use flush cutters to trim the 14-gauge wire to 1.5" (3.8 cm) and make a spiral, as in Step 5, for the top end of the pendant. Make sure you leave a space in the center of the spiral large enough for a large jump ring **(FIGURE 10)**.

15 Open the jump rings with chain-nose pliers (see page 132). Attach a large jump ring through the bottom spiral and dangle charms or perhaps smaller stamped pieces from the bottom, as desired. Attach a large jump ring through the top spiral and thread the pendant on a chain.

10

MAKE IT YOUR OWN

- These dramatic pendants can be quite elaborate—add dangles or layer extra beads for weight and texture.
- If you have trouble finding the perfect focal bead, make one from polymer clay.

DESIGNER * LISA CLAXTON

CRISSCROSS STAMPED & RIVETED EARRINGS

These earrings are the perfect size—large enough to get noticed, yet not overwhelming. The clever crisscross wires are easy to thread through punched holes and add contrast and texture to the stamped silver rectangles. Dangles finish the look.

TECHNIQUES

HOLE PUNCHING P. 24
RIVETING P. 27
OXIDIZING & POLISHING P. 30
STAMPING P. 36

MATERIALS

2 sterling silver 24-gauge rectangular blanks with rounded corners, 9/16" × 15/16" (1.4 cm × 2.3 cm)

1" (2.5 cm) of copper or sterling silver tubing for rivets, 3/32" (2.5 mm) wide

6" (15 cm) of gold-filled 26-gauge wire

4 jump rings, any size and gauge

1 pair ear wires

2 sterling silver charms or dangles

TOOLS

Safety glasses

Permanent fine-tip marker

Metal jeweler's ruler

Screw-down hole punch

Bench block

Design stamps

Stamping hammer

Oxidizing solution

Pro Polish polishing pads or #0000 steel wool and polishing cloth

Tube-cutting pliers

Jeweler's saw

4/0 saw blade

Round needle file or bead reamer tip

Riveting hammer

Flush cutters

Chain-nose pliers

A second pair of chain-nose or flat-nose pliers to aid in opening and closing jump rings

Plastic or rawhide hammer (optional)

FINISHED SIZE

Each earring is 9/16" × 15/16" (1.4 cm × 2.3 cm)

TIPS & TRICKS

- You'll make two sizes of holes in this piece. The larger holes on the top and bottom of the earrings accommodate tube rivets that are applied after all surface embellishment is complete. The smaller holes on the sides of the earrings allow for wire embellishment.
- Use the frame of the screw-down hole punch as a guide for centering the holes on the metal blanks. Align the edge of the blank against the inside wall of the punch to ensure that the blank is straight. Next, use a ruler to measure the amount of metal protruding from each side of the punch.
- Thin metal blanks may bow during stamping. To flatten, place the blank face down on a piece of paper (this protects the blank from scratches on the bench block) and lightly hammer the back of the blank with a plastic or rawhide hammer.

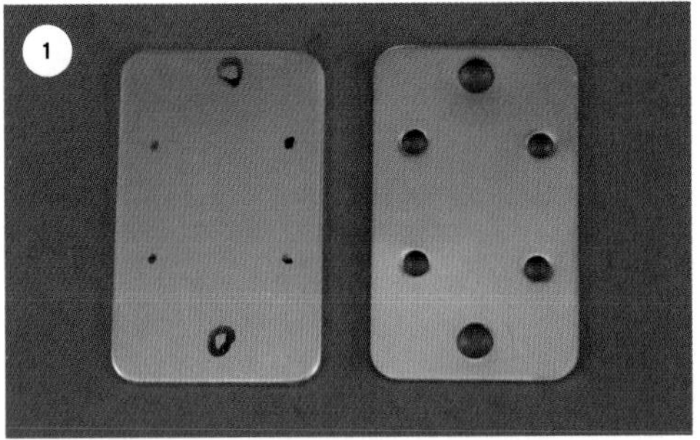

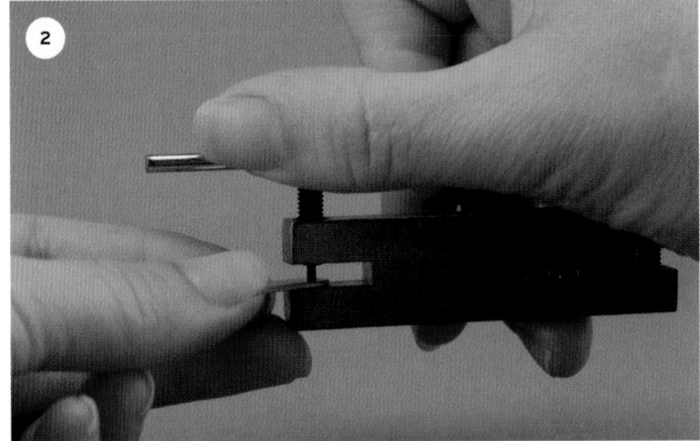

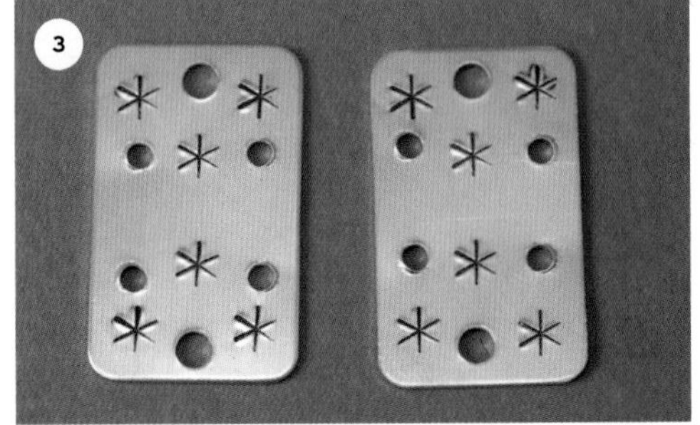

CRISSCROSS STAMPED & RIVETED EARRINGS

1 Use a permanent marker, a ruler, and the screw-down hole punch as a guide to mark holes at the top and bottom of each sterling silver blank for rivets and two holes on each side of the blanks for the wire embellishment.

2 Put on your safety glasses. Using a screw-down hole punch, make all the holes needed for the design (**FIGURE 1**). Punch the top and bottom holes with the larger (12-gauge) side of the screw-down hole punch. Punch the side holes using the smaller (14-gauge) side of the punch (**FIGURE 2**).

3 Place the blanks on a bench block and stamp the blanks with design stamps (**FIGURE 3**). Oxidize and polish the blanks before proceeding.

4 Insert the copper tube in the tube-cutting pliers. Using a jeweler's saw and a 4/0 blade, cut two lengths of tubing for each individual earring (four for the pair) measuring about 2 mm longer than the thickness of the metal blank. Ream out the holes a bit with a round needle file or bead reamer tip if your tube does not fit through.

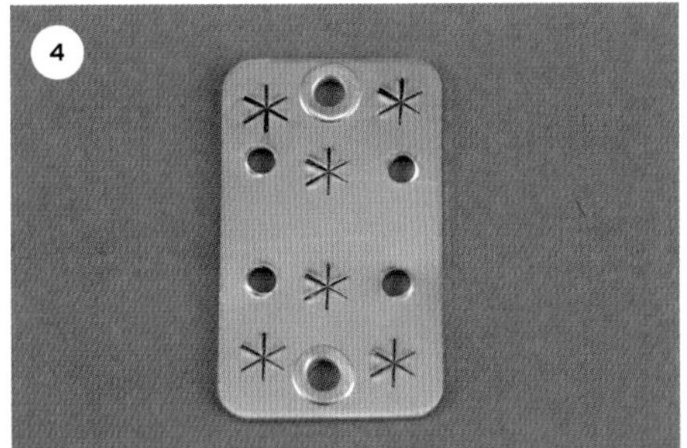

4

5 Rivet the tubes into the top and bottom holes of each earring, as shown on page 27 **(FIGURE 4)**.

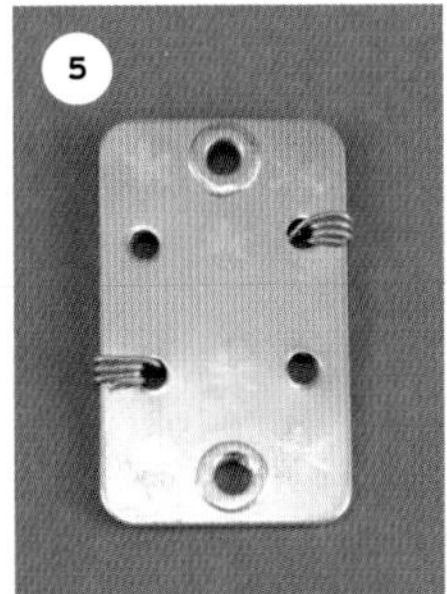

5

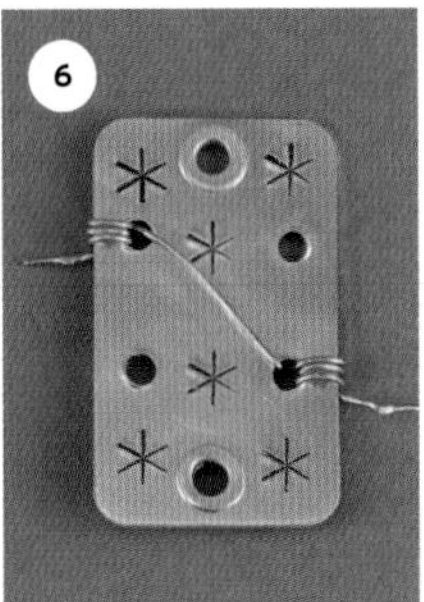

6

6 Using a 3" (7.5 cm) length of 26-gauge wire, attach the wire to the first embellishment hole by wrapping it tightly around the edge of the hole three times. The starting end of the wire should be on the back of the piece pointing toward the outside of the blank edge.

7 Feed the wire across the face of the blank and stitch it through the hole on the opposite and lower side of the blank.

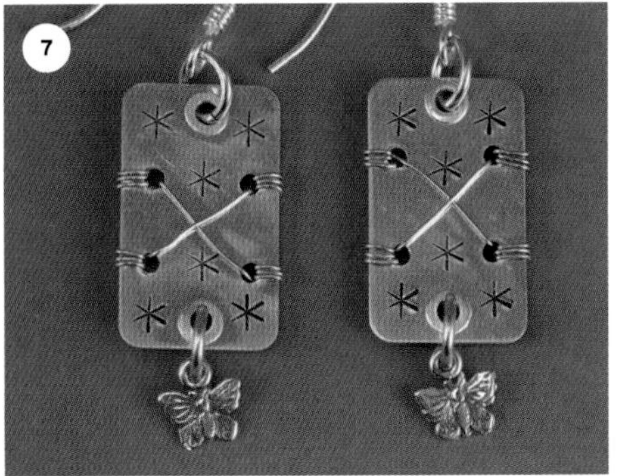

7

8 Wrap the wire three times around the outside of this second hole so that the wire ends on the back, pointing toward the side of the blank edge. **FIGURE 5** shows the back of the blank, and **FIGURE 6** shows the front.

9 With flush cutters, cut the wire tails flush against the piece and repeat the process on the two remaining holes so that the wire embellishment crosses over itself in the middle.

10 Open the jump rings with two pairs of chain-nose pliers (see page 132). Attach the ear wires to the top holes and the charms to the bottom holes **(FIGURE 7)**.

MAKE IT YOUR OWN

- Use contrasting metals as a design element. Mix copper, gold-filled, and sterling silver metals.
- Try the same idea with round or oval blanks.

DESIGNER * KATE FERRANT RICHBOURG

BOLD STAMPED & RIVETED BEADS

These stunning beads are made from four circular metal blanks that are stamped, dapped, stacked, and riveted together with a tube rivet so the beads can be strung. The use of mixed metals is very effective in this design, creating a dramatic look.

TECHNIQUES

HOLE PUNCHING P. 24
DAPPING P. 26
RIVETING P. 27
OXIDIZING & POLISHING P. 30
STAMPING P. 36

MATERIALS

2 round blanks, 24 gauge, $^3/_4$" (2 cm) diameter

2 round blanks, 24 gauge, $^5/_8$" (1.5 cm) diameter

Thin-walled sterling silver tube, 2 mm wide, about 1" (2.5 cm) for each bead

TOOLS

Safety glasses

Circle template

Permanent marker

Hole-punch pliers or drill and drill bits to make a 12-gauge hole

Bench block

Design stamps

Stamping hammer

Oxidizing solution

Pro Polish polishing pads or #0000 steel wool and polishing cloth

Metal dapping block

1-pound brass hammer

Round needle file or bead reamer tip

Tube-cutting pliers

Jeweler's saw

4/0 saw blade

Fine-grit file

Center punch

Plastic or rawhide mallet

Riveting hammer

FINISHED SIZE

Finished size will depend on the size of the blanks used. Beads shown are about $^3/_4$" (2 cm) in diameter at the widest point and about $^5/_8$" (1.5 cm) from hole to hole.

TIPS & TRICKS

- **To make a larger bead, stack six dapped blanks and further stabilize the bead by inserting a flat blank in the middle of the bead.**

BOLD STAMPED & RIVETED BEADS

1 Put on your safety glasses. Measure and make holes in all four metal discs. Use a circle template to find the center, mark the center, and make a hole in each disc using the hole-punch pliers or drill and drill bits **(FIGURE 1)**. The hole for the riveting tube should be slightly smaller than the tube because the hole enlarges when dapped.

2 On the bench block, stamp all four blanks. The smaller top discs can be stamped all over, while the larger discs that go under the top caps can be stamped only around the edges. Stamping must be done *before* shaping the cap with the dapping block. As you stamp, be careful not to hit the edges of the blank and distort them.

3 Oxidize and polish the blanks **(FIGURE 2)**.

4 To dap the blanks, place the blank face down in one well of a dapping block. Choose a rounded dap. Using a 1-pound brass hammer, gently tap the metal dap to curve the metal blank **(FIGURE 3)**. Repeat this process several times, each time progressing to a deeper well and smaller dap. Dap all four discs.

5 Fit all four caps onto the tube. If the tube does not fit through all four holes, enlarge any too-small holes slightly by filing with a round needle file or a bead reamer tip. On either side of the outer holes, mark a 2 mm cutting line on the tube.

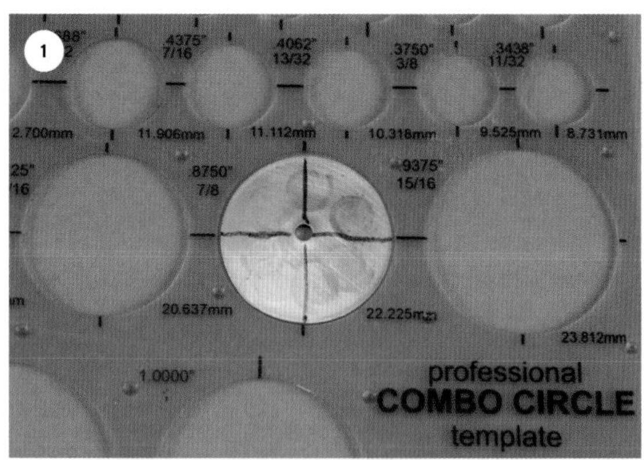

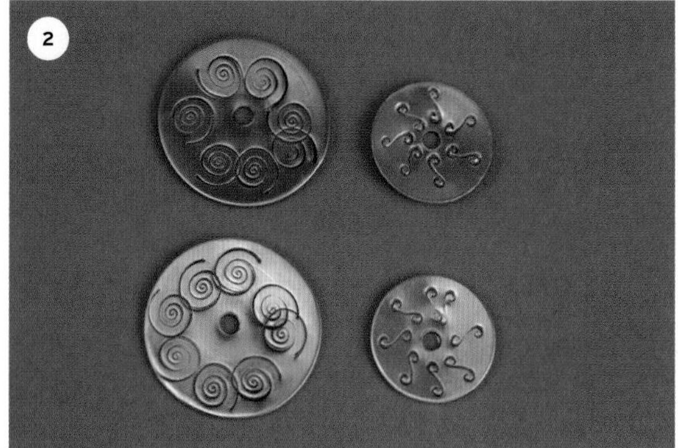

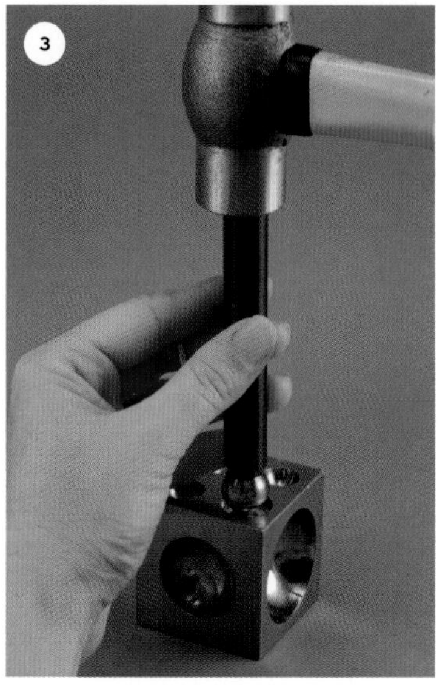

6 Insert the tube in the tube-cutting pliers with the cutting line aligned with the gap in the pliers. Use a jeweler's saw with a 4/0 blade to cut the tube.

7 Layer all of the caps on the cut tube, with two stacked and facing one direction and two facing the other direction, meeting in the center at the widest point. If the dapped blanks do not fit snugly together, file the edges flat with a fine-grit file.

8 Place the bead on the bench block with the tube sitting flush on the block.

9 Place the center punch in the top hole of the tube and tap lightly with a mallet **(FIGURE 4)**. Tap until the top of the tube is slightly flared. Repeat on the opposite side.

10 After flaring both sides of the tube, use the riveting hammer to flatten the tube flush to the cap of the bead. Use light and careful taps and continue this process on both ends of the bead until the tube is flush **(FIGURE 5)**.

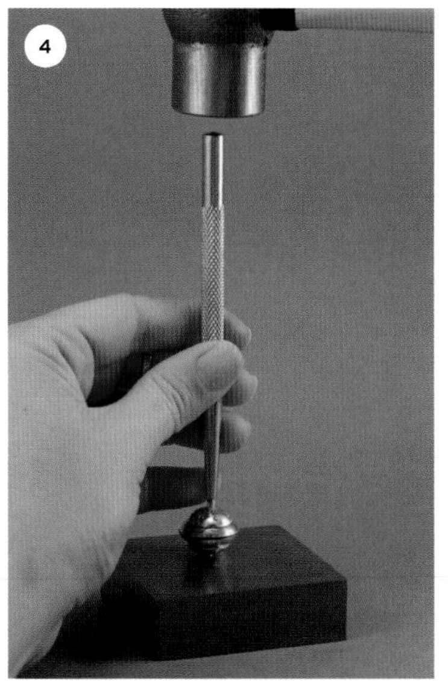

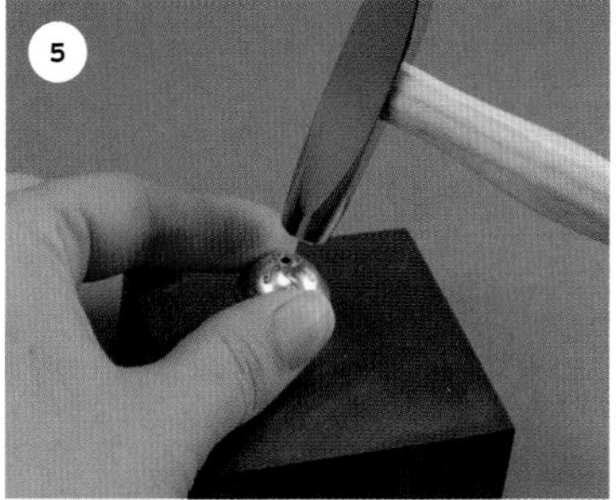

MAKE IT YOUR OWN

- This same process of stamping and dapping circular blanks can be used to make bead caps for your beading projects. Choose a bead that has a hole that will accommodate the tube and dap two blanks that fit the curve of the bead. Rivet the caps to the bead.

DESIGNER * KATE FERRANT RICHBOURG

SNAZZ-IT-UP
PENDANT WITH BAIL

Complete a whimsical stamped pendant with a stamped and riveted bail for perfectly matched style. Not just a fashion statement, a bail will keep your pendant secure and prevent it from flipping over when you wear it.

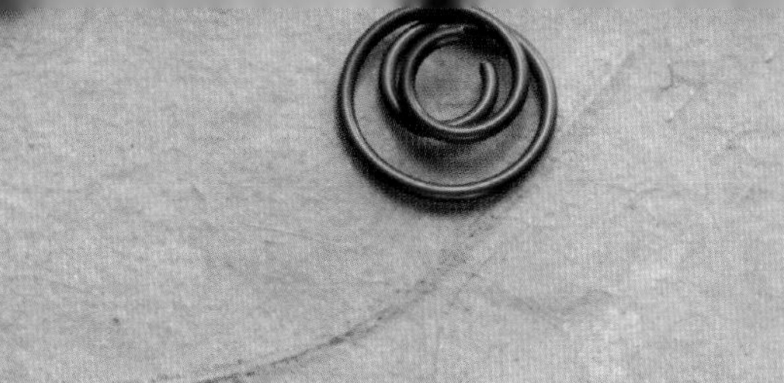

TECHNIQUES

CUTTING & SAWING P. 23
HOLE PUNCHING P. 24
RIVETING P. 27
OXIDIZING & POLISHING P. 30
STAMPING P. 36

MATERIALS

Sterling silver sheet metal, 24-gauge, about 1" x 1/2" (2.5 cm x 1.3 cm) for the bail shown

Sterling silver disc, 24-gauge, 1" (2.5 cm) diameter

Copper disc, 24-gauge, 1/4" (6 mm) diameter

1" (2.5 cm) of sterling silver 14-gauge wire

TOOLS

Bail template

Paper

Scissors

Permanent marker

Metal shears or jeweler's saw and 2/0 saw blade

Small round needle file

Safety glasses

Bench block

Letter/number stamp set and/or design stamps (to make design shown: sun, bird, bull's-eye, dot or period, 19 mm circle)

Stamping hammer

Hole-punch pliers to make 1.8 mm punch

Screw-down hole punch

Riveting hammer

Stepped round-nose pliers

Flush cutters

Oxidizing solution

Pro Polish polishing pads or #0000 steel wool and polishing cloth

FINISHED SIZE

The silver bail shown is 3/8" (1 cm) wide at the top, 1/8" (3 mm) wide at the bottom, 1/8" (3 mm) deep, and 3/8" (1 cm) from top to bottom of the bail, on a 1" (2.5 cm) diameter circular pendant.

TIPS & TRICKS

- **When riveting the bail onto the pendant, hang the loop of the bail over the edge of the bench block so that the bail is not crushed during the riveting process.**

BAIL TEMPLATE

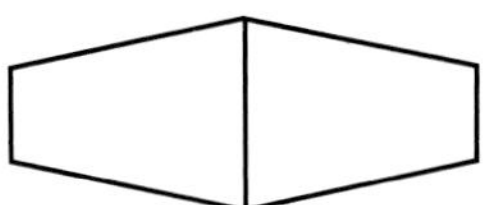

SNAZZ-IT-UP PENDANT WITH BAIL

1 Trace the bail template onto paper and cut out. Using permanent marker, trace around the paper template onto the sterling silver sheet metal. Cut the bail from the metal using metal shears or the jeweler's saw with the 2/0 blade. File the edges.

2 Assemble all pieces for the pendant: sterling silver disc, copper disc, sterling silver bail cut from the template, and wire for riveting.

3 Put on your safety glasses. On the bench block, stamp the sterling silver disc with the 19 mm circle border stamp, the word *tweet*, and dots along the outer border. Mark the top of the circle in the center of the border for placement of the rivet hole for the bail. Punch the hole with the hole-punch pliers **(FIGURE 1)**.

4 Stamp the copper disc with the bull's-eye design and mark the center of the circle for placement of the rivet hole to attach to the pendant. Punch the hole with the small (14-gauge) side of the screw-down hole punch **(FIGURE 1)**.

5 Stamp the sun design in the center front of the bail. Mark the placement of the front hole where you'll rivet the bail to the pendant. Texture the bail using the long end of the riveting hammer in a random pattern **(FIGURES 2 AND 3)**.

6 Punch the marked hole with the hole-punch pliers.

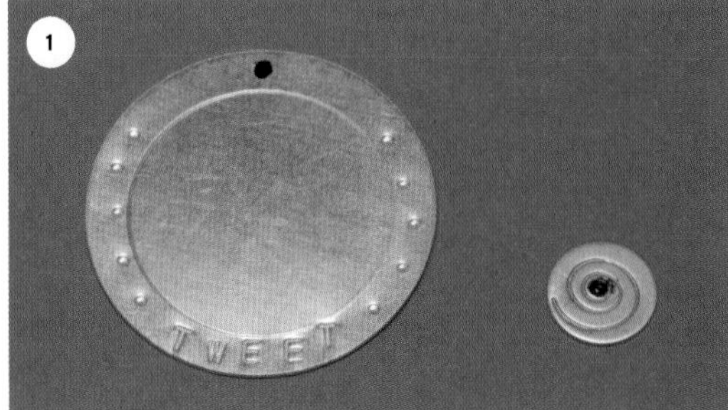

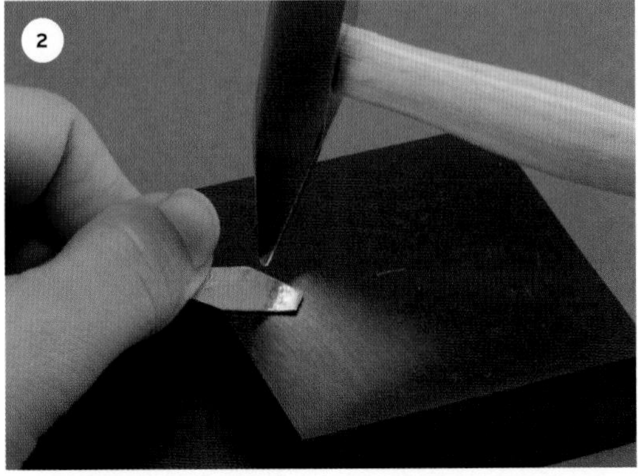

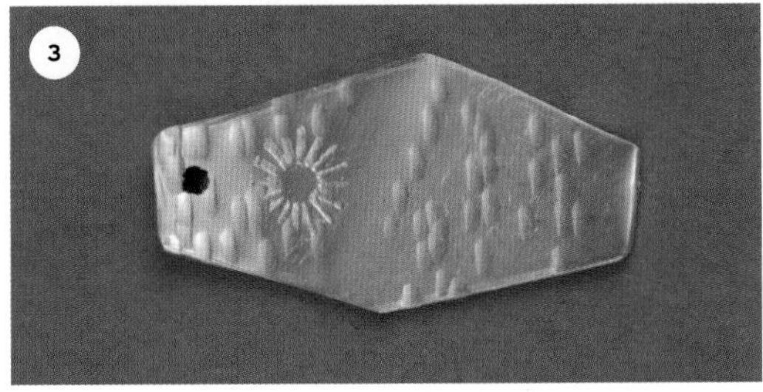

7 Bend the bail in half using your stepped round-nose pliers, using a 4 mm step **(FIGURE 4)**.

8 Using the first hole as a guide, insert the stem of the hole-punch pliers into the hole and punch through the other end of the bail. Squeeze lightly or through some padding to prevent marring the metal with the hole-punch pliers **(FIGURE 5).**

9 Stamp the grass (using a lowercase *l* or the back side of the riveting hammer), dots, and bird on the pendant to complete the scene. Place the copper disc on the silver disc and align the holes for the rivet.

10 Insert the 14-gauge wire through the holes in both discs. Mark the wire on either end about 1 mm beyond the discs and cut the wire with flush cutters. Rivet the wire with the riveting hammer.

11 Insert the pendant between the ends of the bail. Line up the holes in the bail with the hole at the top of the pendant. Squeeze the ends of the bail down onto the pendant to tighten if needed. Insert the wire, mark, and cut a rivet from the 14-gauge wire as before. Rivet the bail to the pendant **(FIGURE 6)**.

12 Oxidize and polish the finished pendant and bail **(FIGURE 7)**. The pendant is ready to hang from a chain or cord of your choice.

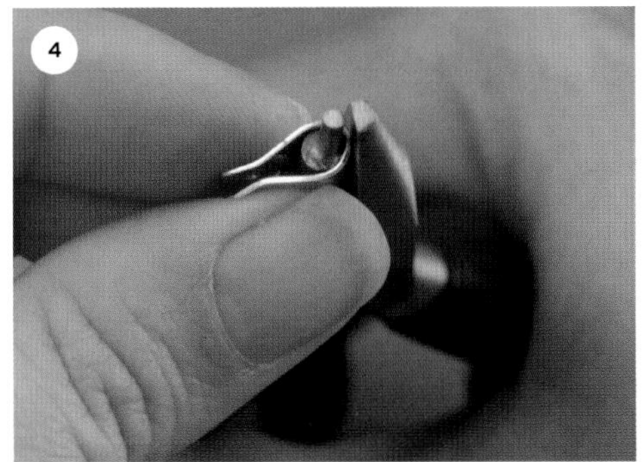
4

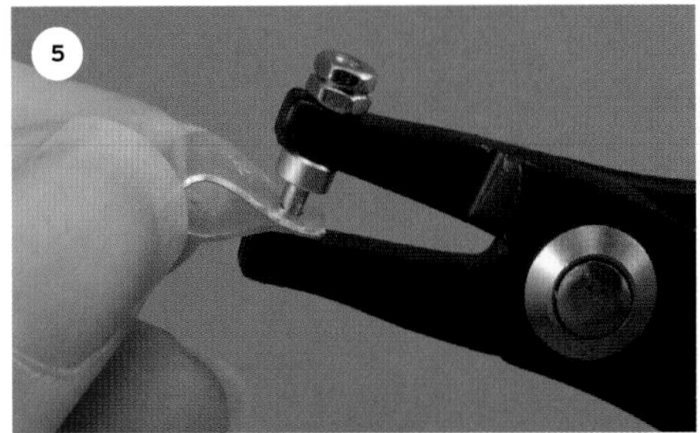
5

6

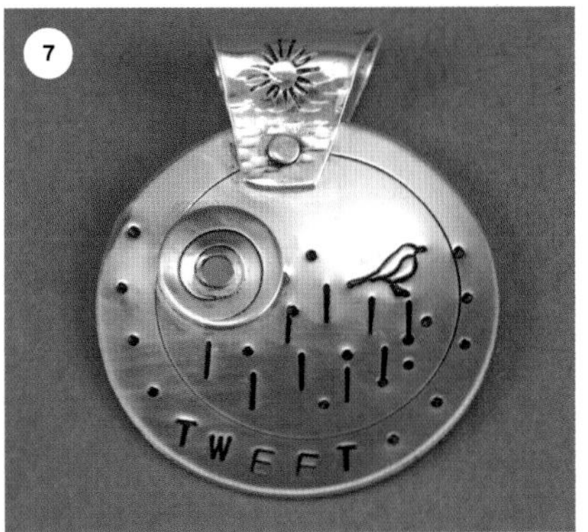

7

MAKE IT YOUR OWN

- Mix metals on your pendants. Try a copper bail with a silver stamped circle and a silver riveting wire.

DESIGNER * TRACY STANLEY

SIMPLY CHARMING

No piece of jewelry is more essential than the charm bracelet; charms can express the wearer's love for favorite places, activities, and symbols. Charm bracelets are beloved classics in the jewelry world, but with imagination and stamping skills, yours can be totally modern.

TECHNIQUES

HAMMERING & TEXTURING P. 22
CUTTING & SAWING P. 23
HOLE PUNCHING P. 24
OXIDIZING & POLISHING P. 30
STAMPING P. 36

MATERIALS

Sterling silver 24-gauge dead-soft sheet metal, about 3" × 3" (7.5 cm × 7.5 cm)

4' (122 cm) of sterling silver 14-gauge dead-soft wire

32 jump rings, 16-gauge, 6mm inner diameter

Mix of 10mm beads

2" (5 cm) head pins to fit through holes of the 10mm beads

Assorted charms to further embellish your bracelet (optional)

1 jump ring, 16-gauge, 7mm inner diameter

TOOLS

Thick paper

Permanent marker or metal scribe

Safety glasses

Metal shears

Metal file

Ring clamp

Letter/number stamp set and/or design stamps

Bench block

Stamping hammer

Screw-down hole punch or hole-punch pliers

Flush cutter to cut wire

Chasing hammer

Round-nose pliers, both short and long

Oxidizing solution

Pro Polish polishing pads or #0000 steel wool and polishing cloth

Chain-nose pliers

A second pair of chain-nose pliers or flat-nose pliers to aid in opening and closing jump rings

FINISHED SIZE

Ocean-themed bracelet shown, 9" (23 cm) long

TIPS & TRICKS

- **To stamp a long word, use smaller-size letters instead of making a bigger charm.**

SIMPLY CHARMING

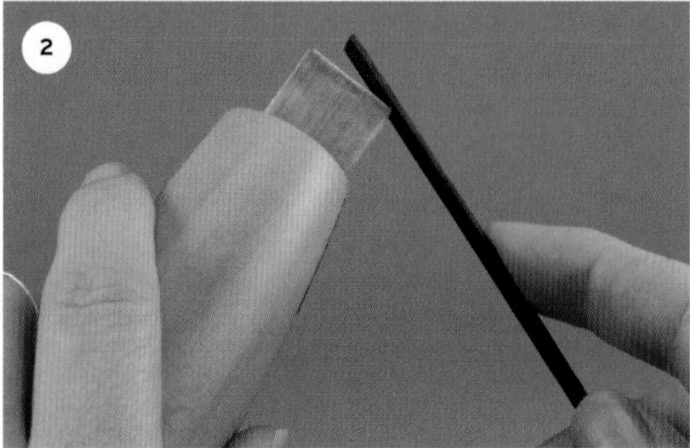

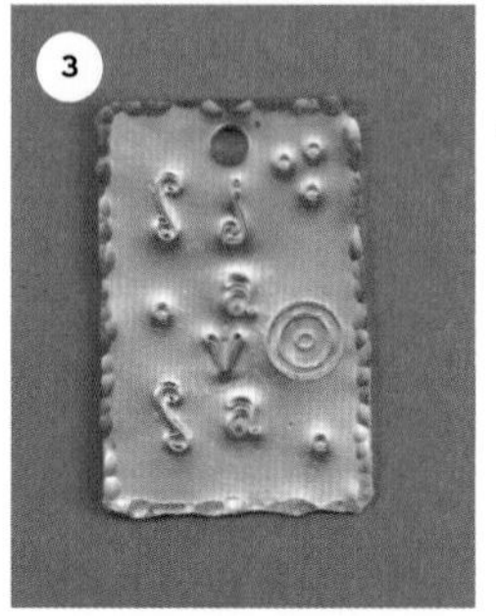

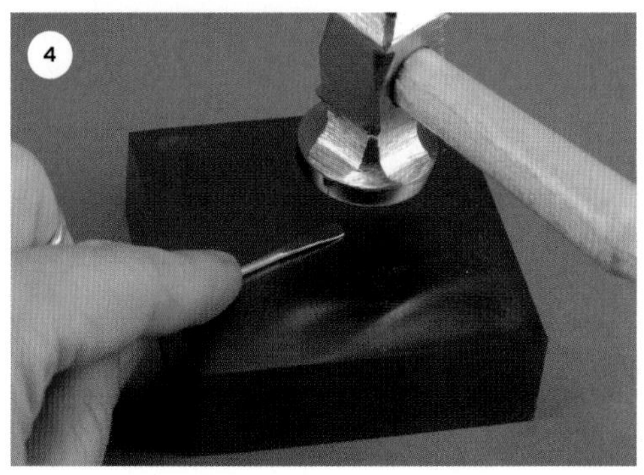

1 To make charms, draw templates on thick paper for each charm you wish to make. Cut the templates out of paper and trace them onto sheet metal with a permanent marker or metal scribe.

2 Put on your safety glasses. Cut out the charms with metal shears **(FIGURE 1)**.

3 File any sharp edges. Hold the pieces in a ring clamp for better leverage while filing **(FIGURE 2)**.

4 Using stamps, bench block and stamping hammer, stamp words and/or designs on the charms as desired.

5 Mark and punch a hole in each charm where you wish to attach it.

6 Lightly hammer the outside edge of the charms using the round end of the chasing hammer **(FIGURE 3)**.

7 To make the chain, use flush cutters to cut a 2¾" (7 cm) piece of 14-gauge wire. Using the chasing hammer, pound both ends of the wire until it is very flat **(FIGURE 4)**.

8 Using the tip of the short round-nose pliers, curl both ends of the wire in opposite directions, one and a half rotations **(FIGURES 5 AND 6)**, to begin the S-hook.

9 Using the base of your long round-nose pliers (where the tool is 4 mm thick), place the wire between the jaws of the pliers with the curl facing you. Turn the pliers away from you, rolling the wire completely over to form a hook **(FIGURE 7)**. Repeat on the other side.

10 Hammer the top of the curve with the chasing hammer **(FIGURE 8)**. Repeat on the other side. Hammering is likely to open the curve a bit—use the chain-nose pliers to pull it back closed.

5

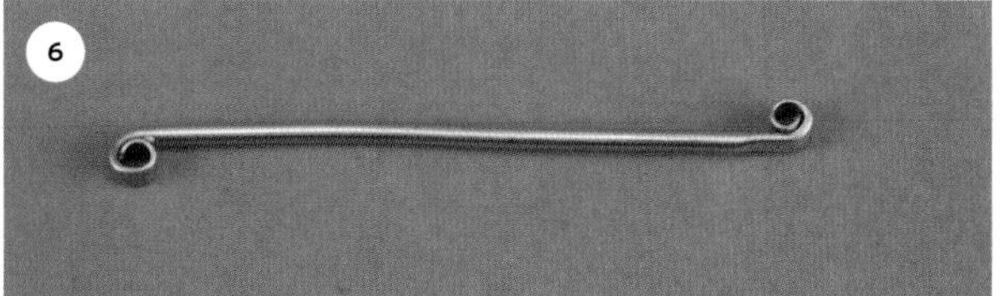
6

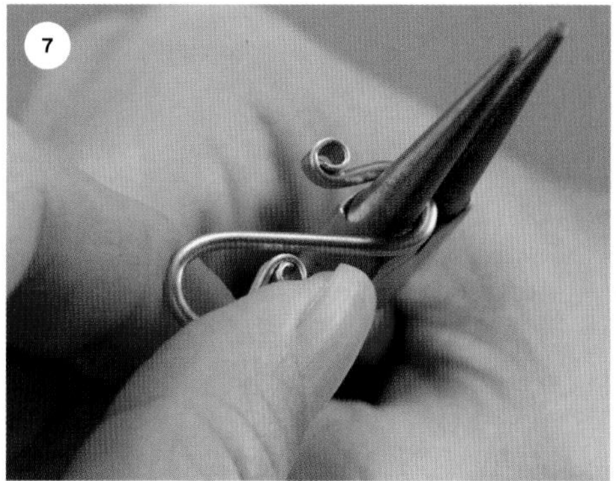
7

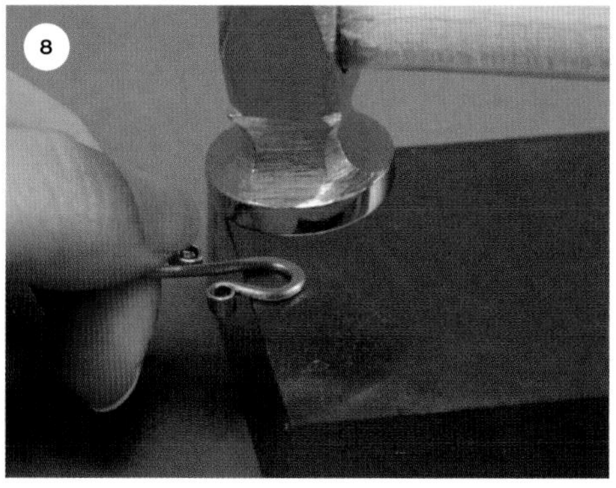
8

11 Make as many S-hooks as needed for the length of bracelet desired. A bracelet with eight S-hooks will measure about 8½" (21.5 cm) long; a bracelet with nine S-hooks will measure about 9" (23 cm) long.

12 Oxidize and polish all components, including the chain and any new charms, before linking them together.

13 Open the jump rings with chain-nose pliers, using a second pair of chain-nose pliers or a pair of flat-nose pliers to aid (see page 132). Connect the links with 16-gauge jump rings **(FIGURE 9)**.

14 Attach the charms on the same side of the chain **(FIGURE 10)**.

15 Make embellishing dangles by putting a bead on a head pin and wire-wrapping it to the chain (see page 133).

16 Further embellish by adding pre-made charms with jump rings.

17 The last link of your S-hook link serves as the clasp. Open one end slightly. Add the 7mm inner diameter jump ring to the other side to act as the eye of the clasp.

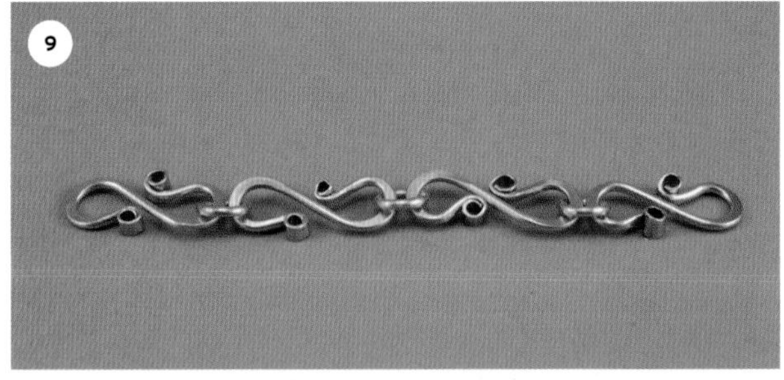

MAKE IT YOUR OWN

- Create a theme for your bracelet. Try making charms for a coffee theme, a beach theme, or a travel theme.

CHARMED, I'M SURE! IDEAS FOR CHARM BRACELETS

The charm-bracelet tradition dates back thousands of years. Modern charm bracelets grew popular at the end of World War II, as soldiers picked up trinkets made by European artisans to bring home to their wives, sisters, and girlfriends.

Today, charm bracelets are enjoying new popularity as one of the most unique and personal pieces of jewelry that a girl or woman can own. Charm bracelets transcend age—they're as appropriate for young girls as they are for their moms!

I have a friend with a charm bracelet for each decade in her life; she's now completing her fifth bracelet.

With the stamping techniques in this book, it's easy to make your own charms. The bracelet you make today will become an heirloom for the next generation.

Here are some popular charm-bracelet themes to start your creative wheels turning:

TRAVEL

Collect charms that represent the region you're visiting.

HOBBIES

Make charms that reflect your interest in sports, quilting, knitting, cooking, pets, yoga, sailing, or anything else you're enthusiastic about.

HOLIDAYS

New Year's, Christmas, Halloween, Day of the Dead—every holiday has images and words that you can stamp for a special bracelet.

GRANDMOTHER'S BRACELET

For a bracelet for my mom, I stamped charms that each had the name of a grandchild. As each child grows and reveals more personality, I'll add to it with stamped charms that reflect their interests.

DESIGNER * TRACY STANLEY

RIVETED COLLAGE
PENDANT

A fairly large piece of metal, textured with design stamps, serves as the foundation for a necklace that will get you noticed. Rivet contrasting metal shapes to the base in a metal "collage" and send the world an inspiring message!

TECHNIQUES

CUTTING & SAWING P. 23
HOLE PUNCHING P. 24
RIVETING P. 27
OXIDIZING & POLISHING P. 30
STAMPING P. 36

MATERIALS

Copper sheet metal, 24-gauge, 1" × 2$^{1}/_{16}$" (2.5 cm × 5.2 cm) or enough to cut desired shape

Sterling silver sheet metal, 24-gauge, dead-soft, $^{3}/_{8}$" × 1$^{1}/_{4}$" (1 cm × 3.1 cm) and $^{5}/_{8}$" × $^{7}/_{16}$" (1.6 cm × 1.1 cm) or enough to cut desired shape

Copper round wire, 14-gauge, enough for 4 rivets or as many as desired

1 silver or copper jump ring, 18-gauge, 4mm

TOOLS

Paper

Permanent marker

Metal shears

Safety glasses

Chasing hammer

Bench block

Letter/number stamp set and/or design stamps

Stamping hammer

Texturing tools

Plastic mallet

Metal file

Screw-down hole punch, hole-punch pliers, or drill and drill bits to make holes for 14-gauge wire

Pro Polish polishing pads or #0000 steel wool and polishing cloth

Oxidizing solution

Flush cutters

Riveting hammer

Chain-nose pliers

A second pair of chain-nose or flat-nose pliers to aid in opening and closing jump ring

FINISHED SIZE

Pendant shown is 1" × 2$^{1}/_{16}$" (2.5 cm × 5.2 cm)

TIPS & TRICKS

- Begin this project by designing your pendant. Any size and any shape will work, but keep it simple. Draw your design on a piece of paper to see the actual size; if you use a thick piece of paper, you can even press the stamps into the paper to practice the spacing.
- For an added design element, substitute tube rivets for wire rivets.

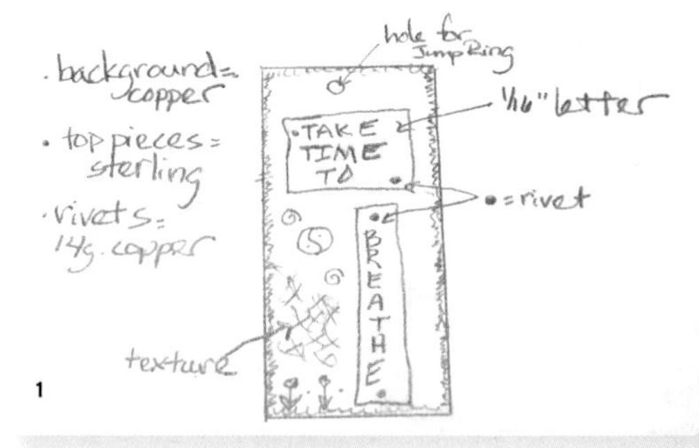

RIVETED COLLAGE PENDANT

1 Design and plan out your pendant design on a piece of paper **(FIGURE 1)**.

2 Draw the pendant background shape onto the copper sheet metal with a permanent marker and cut out the shape using metal shears **(FIGURE 2)**.

3 Put on your safety glasses. Tap around the edges of the metal using the ball end of your chasing hammer to smooth out the edges and create a framed look around the piece **(FIGURE 3)**.

4 Draw boxes on the background piece to indicate where the top pieces will lie. On the bench block, stamp and/or texture around those boxes. Cut and stamp or texture the top pieces from the sterling silver sheet metal **(FIGURE 4)**. Make sure you plan the position of the riveting holes so you don't cut and stamp only to have no place for the rivets.

5 Flatten the stamped metal pieces with the plastic mallet as needed and file the edges of the metal to eliminate any sharp points.

6 With a screw-down hole punch or hole-punch pliers, punch a hole in the top of the background piece of metal to be used to add a jump ring.

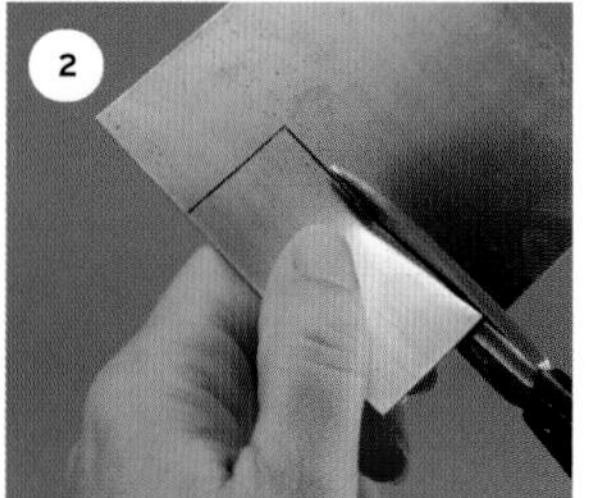

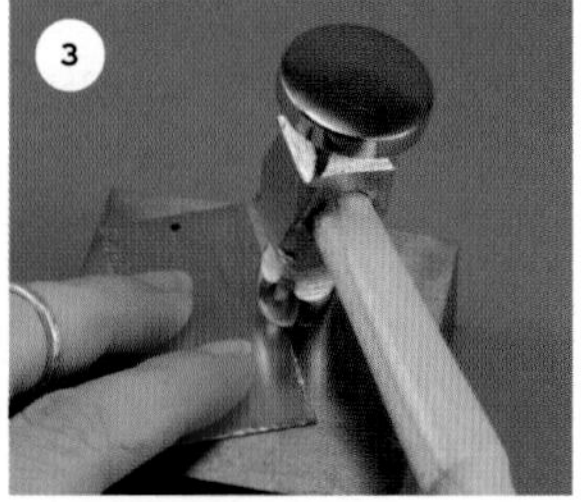

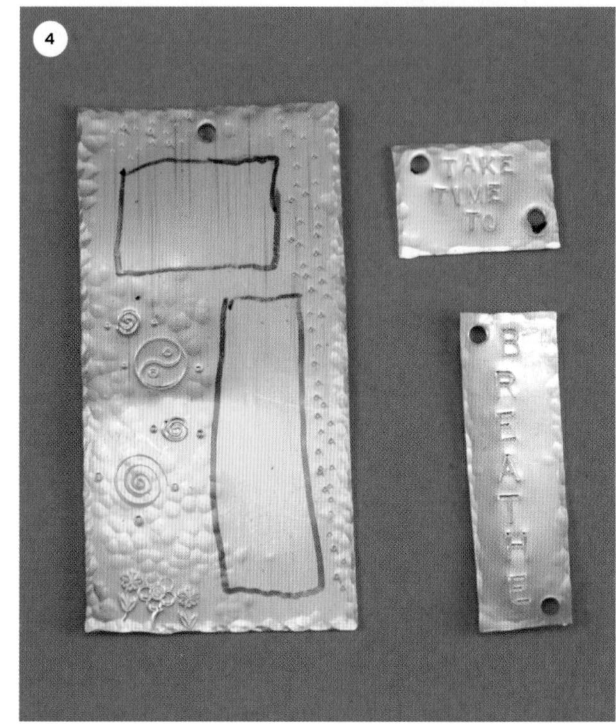

7 Use a polishing pad or steel wool to remove the pen marks, then oxidize and polish the pieces.

8 Finish the corners and edges as described in Step 3.

9 Mark and punch holes in the top pieces. Drill or punch holes appropriate for a 14-gauge wire rivet.

10 Lay the top pieces on the background piece in the desired positions and mark through the holes to indicate where to punch the background metal **(FIGURE 5)**.

11 Punch the bottom holes. Insert the copper wire into the two holes, cut with flush cutters, and use a riveting hammer to rivet the top pieces onto the background.

12 Use two pairs of chain-nose pliers to open the jump ring, insert it into the top hole, and close. The pendant is ready to hang from a chain or cord of your choice **(FIGURE 6)**.

MAKE IT YOUR OWN

- Try layering metals—sterling onto copper, as shown here, or vice versa—or varying the rivet wires to add a design element.
- Use round shapes to give your collage pendant a different silhouette.

DESIGNER * CONNIE FOX

FULL CIRCLE BRACELET

Stamping with various circular shapes gives this daring design its name. Use 20-gauge dead-soft sheet metal in sterling silver, copper, or brass for the bracelet components for easy stamping and shaping. Express your own style by adding beads and other components to the design.

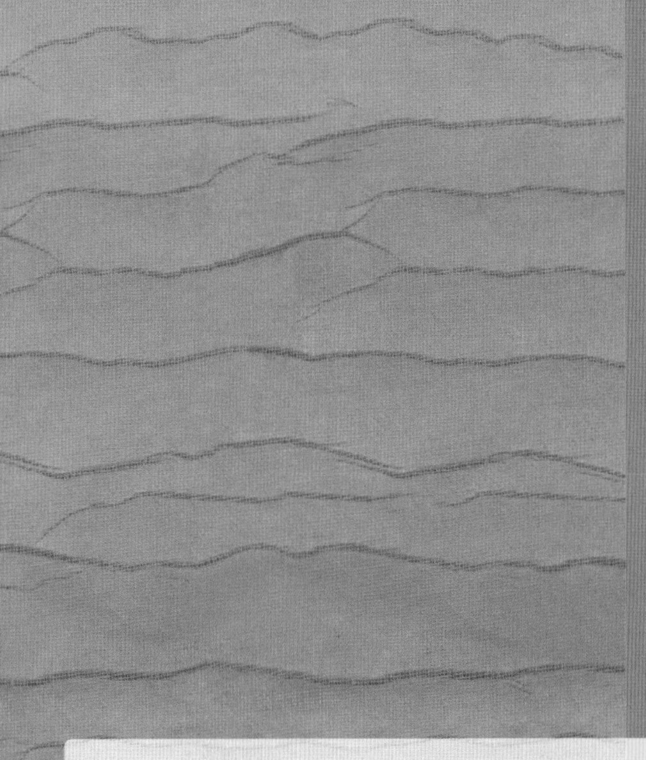

TECHNIQUES

CUTTING & SAWING P. 23
HOLE PUNCHING P. 24
OXIDIZING & POLISHING P. 30
STAMPING P. 36

MATERIALS

10 jump rings, 16-gauge, 6mm inner diameter

5 jump rings, 16-gauge, 5mm inner diameter (for clasp)

20-gauge dead-soft sheet metal in sterling silver, copper, or brass, 1.5" wide × 7" long (3.8 cm × 17.8 cm) for a 6" (15.2 cm) wrist

1$^5/_8$" (4.1 cm) square 8-gauge brass wire for toggle bar

4 mini hex-head bolts

2 flat brass disc beads with small holes

Decorative glass beads, similar to those shown:

- a $^5/_8$" diameter × $^1/_8$" deep (1.5cm x 3mm) flat circle with a center hole (shown in mustard, white, and brown)
- an organically shaped oval bead that is $^7/_8$" wide × 1" high (2.2 cm × 2.5 cm) with a center hole (shown in mustard and brown)
- a squared-off donut shape that is about $^3/_4$" wide × 1" high x $^1/_8$" deep (1.9cm × 2.5cm x 3mm) (shown in brown and white)

3" (7.5 cm) length of 16-gauge wire

TOOLS

Card stock

Scissors

Center punch

Chain-nose pliers

A second pair of chain-nose or flat-nose pliers to aid in opening and closing jump ring

Sandpaper in 200, 400, and 600 grits

Permanent marker

Metal scribe (optional)

Safety glasses

Jeweler's saw

2/0 saw blades

Metal shears

Half-round hand file

Bench block

Design stamps

Stamping hammer

Flexible-shaft machine, high-speed rotary tool, or drill press

High-speed twist drill bits #37, #46, and #53

Disc cutter to create large hole for toggle (optional)

Bracelet-bending pliers

Triangle-shaped file

Oxidizing solution

Pro Polish polishing pads or #0000 steel wool and polishing cloth

2 EZ socket wrenches for small hex-head bolts

Flush cutters

Riveting hammer (optional)

Clear nail polish (optional)

FINISHED SIZE

7$^5/_8$" long × 1$^1/_2$" wide (19.3 cm × 3.8 cm)

TIPS & TRICKS

- **Always make paper templates for a better fit and fewer mistakes.**
- **When shaping metal with drilled holes, the holes can become distorted, and your bolts or jump rings will not fit in the holes. If this happens, drill through the holes with a #53 drill bit.**
- **When curving sheet metal components with the bracelet-bending pliers, squeeze the metal multiple times along the length and across the width. Because the sheet metal is wide, you'll need to "bite away" with the pliers to ensure that the entire component curves.**

FULL CIRCLE BRACELET

1 Make templates from card stock for the components of your bracelet. My large-scale bracelet components are 1³⁄₈" to 1⁵⁄₈" (3.5 cm to 4 cm) in height and ⁵⁄₈" to 1³⁄₄" (1.5 cm to 4.3 cm) in width. The toggle hole is ³⁄₄" (2 cm) in diameter. Choose the size of your bracelet components to suit your style.

2 Punch small holes in the card stock for jump rings and attachments **(FIGURE 1)**. The rectangular bead is held by a staple; see Step 16 for more information. See Step 9 for measurement requirements for the toggle clasp. Punch or cut out a hole that is ³⁄₄" (2 cm) in diameter to receive the toggle bar. Rather than making a paper bar, consider making the actual toggle bar first and attaching it to your card-stock bracelet.

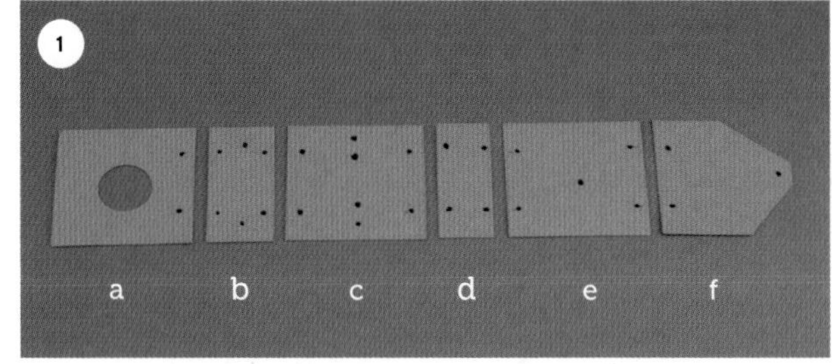

Component dimensions, left to right:

a Square with large circle cut out of center: 1¹⁄₂" (3.8 cm) square

b Rectangle ⁵⁄₈" × 1¹⁄₂" (1.5 cm × 3.8 cm)

c Rectangle 1" × 1¹⁄₂" (2.5 cm × 3.8 cm)

d Rectangle ⁵⁄₈" × 1¹⁄₂" (1.5 cm × 3.8 cm)

e Square 1³⁄₈" × 1¹⁄₂" (3.5 cm × 3.8 cm)

f Arrow 1¹⁄₄" (3.2 cm) at widest point x 1⁵⁄₈" (4 cm)

3 Open all the jump rings with chain-nose pliers, using a second pair of chain-nose pliers or flat-nose pliers to aid in the process (see page 132). Join the card-stock components with 16-gauge, 6mm inner diameter jump rings. Use 16-gauge, 5mm inner diameter jump rings to join the bar to the bracelet. Adjust your components until you get a good fit and a pleasing design.

4 Clean the sheet metal with sandpaper to remove scratches. Start with the coarsest grit and then finish with the medium and fine grits.

5 Use the permanent marker or a scribe to trace the outline of your template onto the sheet metal.

6 Put on your safety glasses. Cut the shapes using a jeweler's saw and a 2/0 blade. You can also cut your shapes with metal shears. File the edges until smooth with the half-round file.

7 On the bench block, stamp the metal using designs of your choice **(FIGURE 2)**. I used a center punch, nail sets filed flat, circle-shaped design stamps, and a chasing tool. You can stamp random, geometric, or repeating patterns **(FIGURE 3)**.

8 Using your templates again, mark where the holes are to be drilled. Center punch at the marks. Use a #53 high-speed twist drill to create the holes. Remove burrs from the back of the sheet metal by reaming them with a large drill bit (I used a #37) or a file.

9 The bar for a secure toggle clasp must be a little more than twice the size of the diameter of the toggle hole. My bar is 1$^{5}/_{8}$" (4.1 cm) and the loop hole diameter is $^{13}/_{16}$" (2 cm). Using a disc cutter

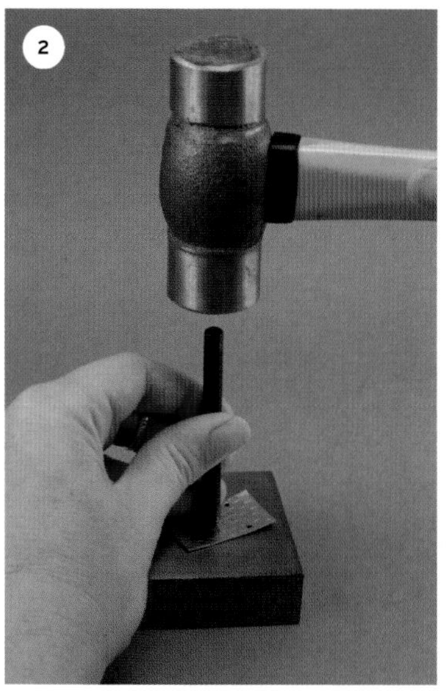
2

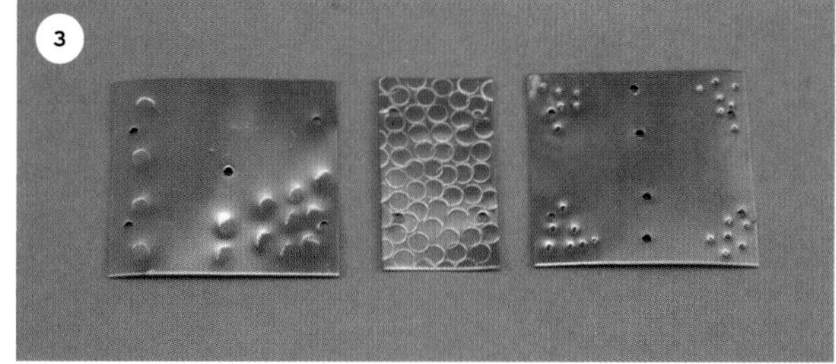
3

or a jeweler's saw with a 2/0 blade, create a hole in the sheet metal for the toggle bar. Saw the bar from the 8-gauge square wire with the jeweler's saw and a 2/0 blade.

10 Center punch and drill a pilot hole in the middle of the toggle bar wire using a #53 drill bit. Drill in the same hole with a #46 drill bit. File the ends of the bar and the inner circle until smooth.

11 Curve each component to contour to your wrist using bracelet-bending pliers.

12 Use a triangle file to file triangle shapes into the edge of one of your components **(FIGURE 4)**.

13 Oxidize and polish all components.

14 Using miniature bolts, join the remaining beads and metal beads to the base of the bracelet. Secure the bolts using two EZ socket wrenches, one for the hex head and one for the nut **(FIGURE 5)**.

15 With flush cutters or the jeweler's saw, cut or saw off the end of the bolts, leaving about 1 to 2 mm. Either rivet the ends carefully **(FIGURE 6)** with a riveting hammer or file them down and use a dab of clear nail polish to secure the bolt.

16 The rectangular bead in the sample was joined to the bracelet component by making two staples from the 16-gauge round wire. The shape is the same as a standard staple, but with longer prongs. Drill two holes to accommodate the prongs of the staple. Introduce the staple from the back of the sheet metal and use chain-nose pliers to pull the legs of the staple forward and wrap them around the bead. Repeat for the second staple **(FIGURES 7 AND 8)**.

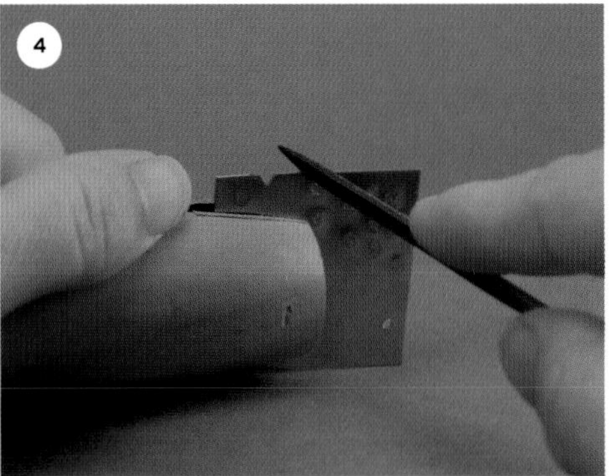
4

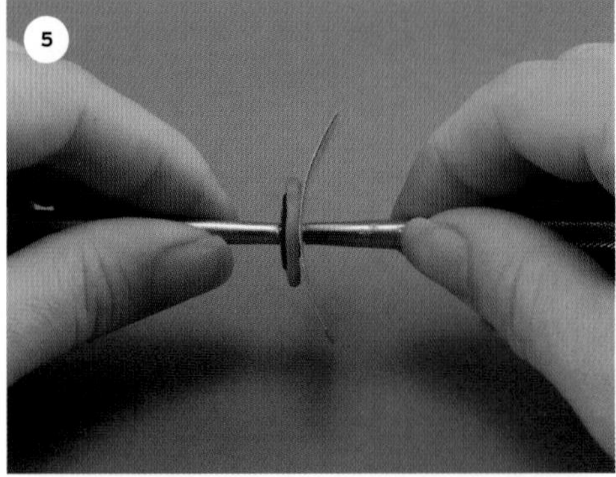
5

6

17 Join the metal components with the jump rings. Join the toggle bar to the end of the bracelet.

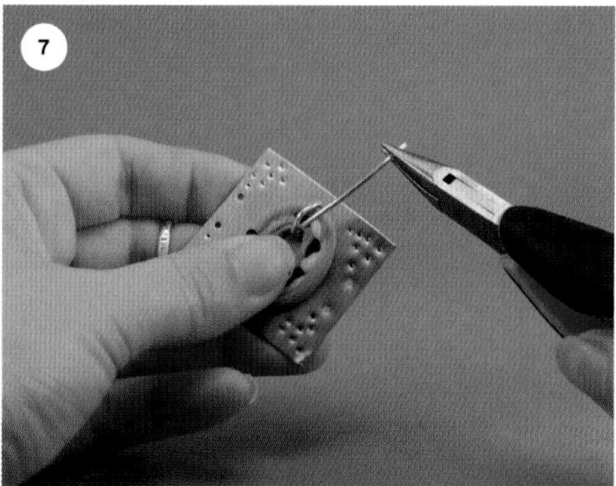

MAKE IT YOUR OWN

- Any shapes and designs will work in this project. Get creative and daring with your jeweler's saw and make personalized shapes.

GALLERY

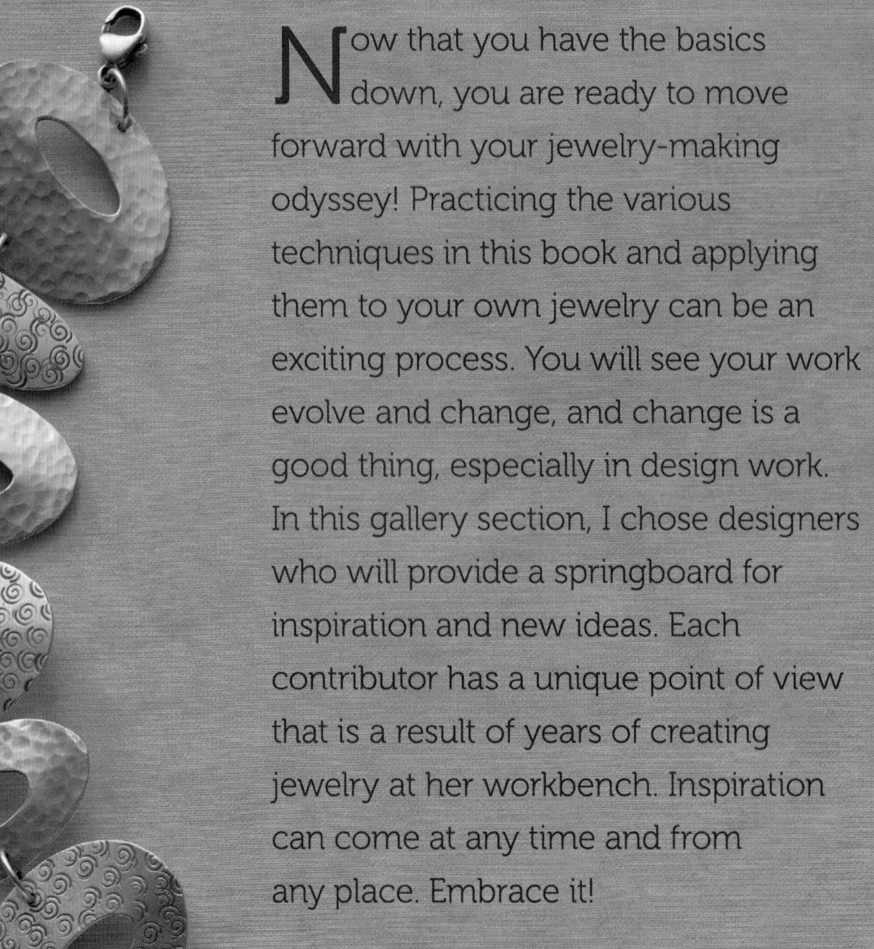

Now that you have the basics down, you are ready to move forward with your jewelry-making odyssey! Practicing the various techniques in this book and applying them to your own jewelry can be an exciting process. You will see your work evolve and change, and change is a good thing, especially in design work. In this gallery section, I chose designers who will provide a springboard for inspiration and new ideas. Each contributor has a unique point of view that is a result of years of creating jewelry at her workbench. Inspiration can come at any time and from any place. Embrace it!

INFINITY
Lisa Dienst-Thomas
Sterling silver
8" × 1½" (20.5 cm × 3.8 cm)

This modern bracelet links together oval donut shapes cut from sterling silver. The artist alternated design stamps and texturing for visual interest.

ETERNITY
Lisa Dienst-Thomas
Sterling silver, fused glass
$19^1/_2$" × $1^1/_2$" (49.5 cm × 3.8 cm)

Graceful spirals stamped onto the base of this stunning pendant echo the patterns in the fused glass focal component. Periwinkle beads and wrapped wire create a contemporary mix of color and texture.

SEEK LOVE
Randi Samuels
Sterling silver, copper
7⅝" × ½" (19.2 cm × 1.3 cm)

Subtle stamping around the edges of two pieces of cut sheet metal, connected with contrasting rivets, makes a meaningful bracelet. The heart dangle adds a sweet finish to the clasp.

FLOWER POWER
Lori Ramotar
Sterling silver, copper
2⅜" (5.7 cm) diameter

Just one rivet holds together multiple layers of stamped metal and silver spacer beads. A stamped flower toggle clasp completes the look.

SPIRAL RINGS
Lisa Claxton
Fine silver
1/8" to 1/2" wide (3 mm to 13 mm)

These spiral rings incorporate different stamped designs or textures as the metal curves into a new rotation. The variations in the stamped designs make for complex and fascinating rings.

BE STILL
Lisa Leonard
Sterling silver
3/4" x 3/4" (2 cm x 2 cm)

Simple stamping has maximum impact in this delightful bird-on-a-branch design. The square shape and graphic branch design add sophistication.

SWEETHEART TREE
Lisa Leonard
Sterling silver
1 1/4" x 1 1/8" (3.2 cm x 3 cm)

Instead of carving initials in wood, stamp them on metal for a memento of young love. Stamping can create life-like textures, as in the tree trunk in this pendant.

RIVETED TEXT
Randi Samuels
Sterling silver, copper
8½" circumference ×
½" wide (21.5 cm × 1.3 cm)

Strips cut from sheet metal are riveted together with stamped words and textures to make inspiring bangle bracelets to wear alone or together.

ELEMENTS
Lisa Niven Kelly
Sterling silver, gemstones, Bali silver beads, freshwater pearls
Pendant: 2¾" × 2¾" (7 cm × 7 cm)

Freshwater pearls are an unexpected element in this dramatic three-piece pendant with the artist's signature textured edging. Stamping ties the three components together and adds depth to each section.

DESSERT FIRST
Lori Ramotar
Sterling silver, brass
$2^{1}/_{8}$" × $1^{1}/_{4}$"
(5.2 cm × 3.2 cm)

Everybody's favorite motto becomes a jewelry treat with textured and stamped silver and a stamped brass "cone." Let the artist's inventiveness inspire you to cut your own shapes from sheet metal.

DANCE
Lisa Niven Kelly
Sterling silver, seed beads, leather
$6^{1}/_{4}$" × $^{3}/_{4}$" (16 cm × 2 cm)

This cuff mixes sparkling beads, textured leather, and a bold silver centerpiece with a daring message for an accessory that makes every day a party.

BASIC WIREWORK TECHNIQUES

Crimping

Crimp tubes are seamless metal tubes used to secure the end of a beading wire. To use, string a crimp tube and the connection finding (i.e., the loop of the clasp). Pass the wire back through the crimp tube, leaving a short tail. Use the back notch of the crimping pliers to press the length of the tube down between the wires, enclosing them in separate chambers of the crescent shape. Rotate the tube 90 degrees and use the front notch of the pliers to fold the two chambers onto themselves, forming a clean cylinder. Trim the excess wire.

1

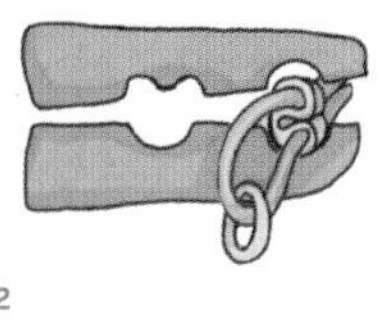

2

Crimping Cover

Crimp covers hide crimp tubes and give a professional finish. To attach, gently hold a crimp cover in the front notch of the crimping pliers. Insert the crimped tube and gently squeeze the pliers, encasing the crimp tube inside the cover.

1

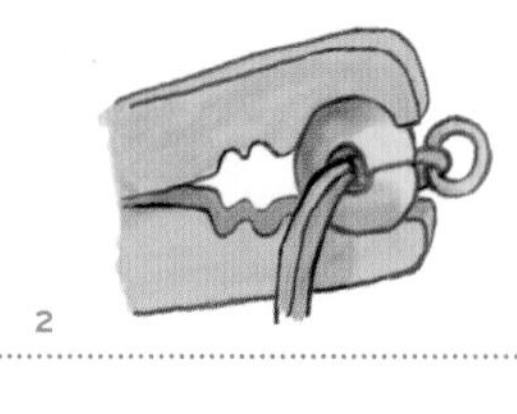

2

3

S-hook

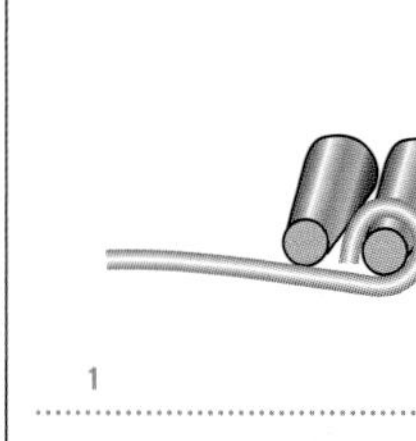

1

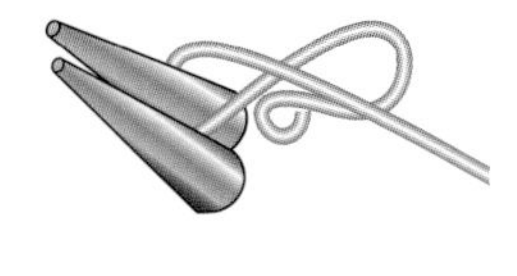

2

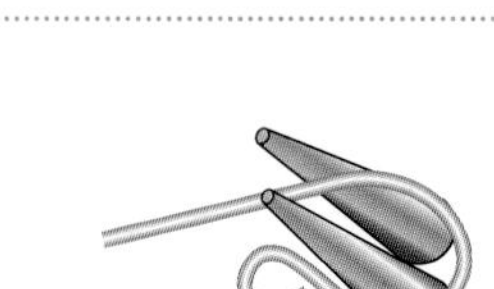

3

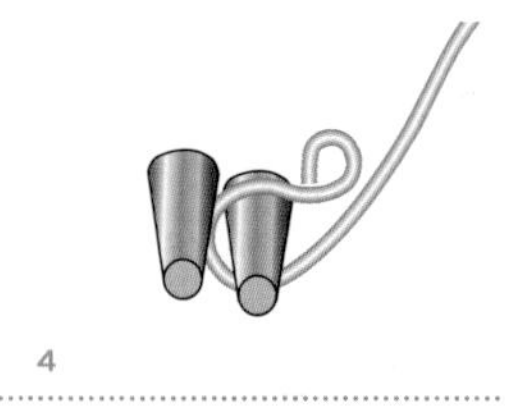

4

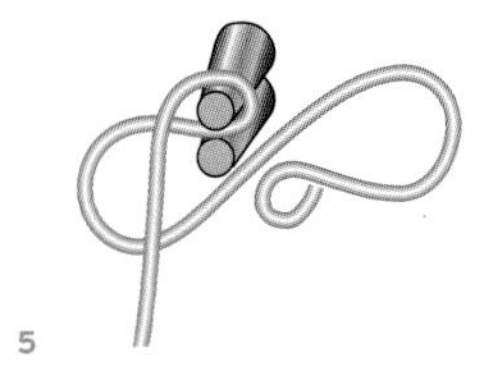

5

Opening & Closing Jump Rings

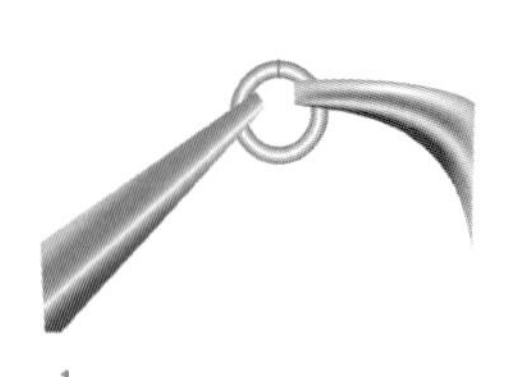

1

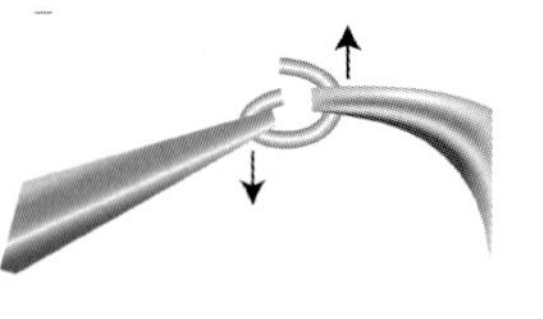

2

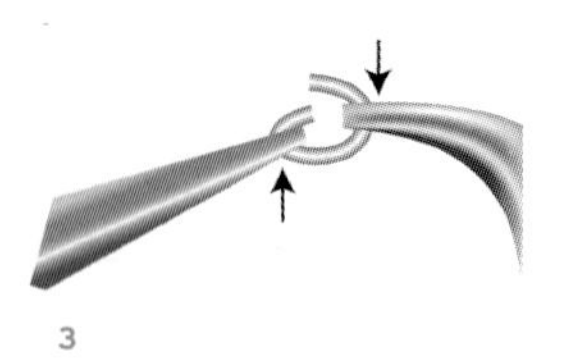

3

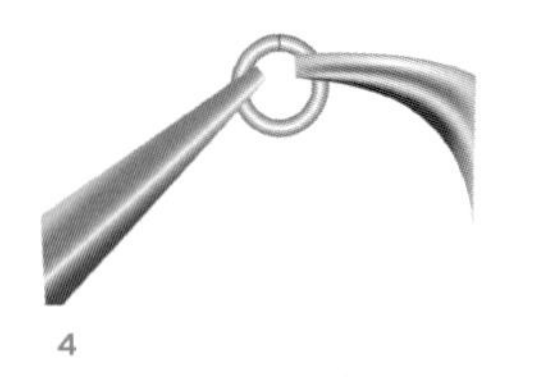

4

Wire Wrapped Loop

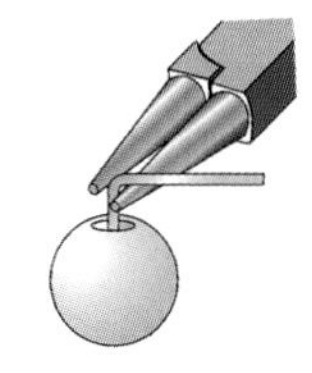

1

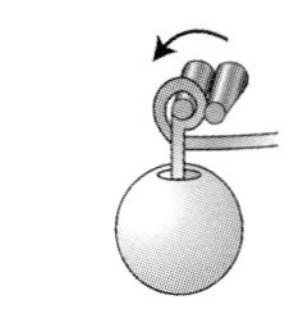

4

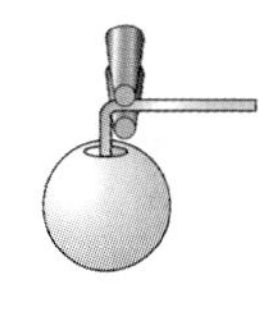

2

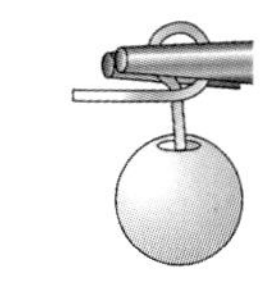

5

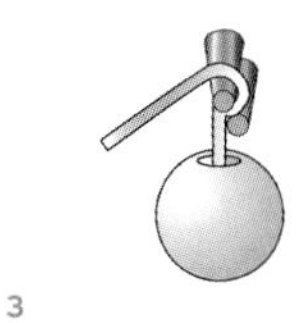

3

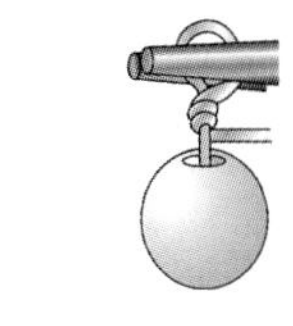

6

Spirals

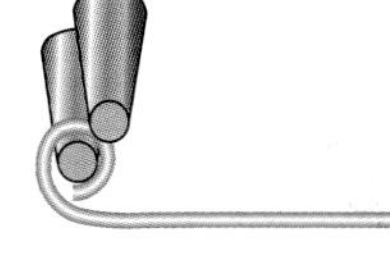

1

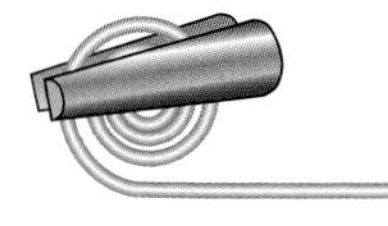

2

Simple Loops

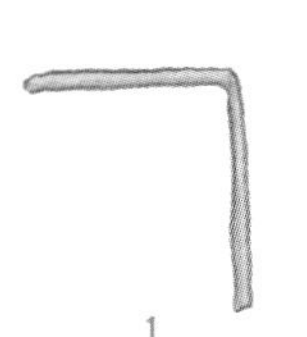

1

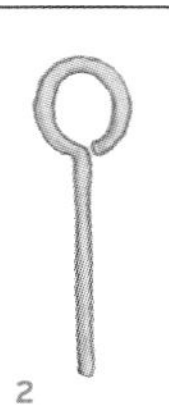

2

Wire Gauge Chart

gauge	round	half-round	square
2g			
3g			
4g			
6g			
7g			
8g			
9g			
10g			
11g			
12g			
13g			
14g			
16g			
18g			
19g			
20g			
21g			
22g			
24g			
26g			

CONTRIBUTORS

Janice Berkebile **wiredarts.net**

Janice Berkebile of Bothell, Washington, is inspired by the organic forms found in nature, Japanese motifs, textiles techniques, and the sinuous lines of the Art Nouveau movement. Janice's focus is wire and metalwork. Janice is a partner in Wired Arts with Tracy Stanley.

Lisa Claxton **lisaclaxton.blogspot.com**

Lisa Claxton was first attracted to seed beads as a teenager, and today she explores all forms of jewelry making. Most recently, she has focused on personal expression during the creative process. Lisa currently resides in bead-friendly Berkeley, California. She teaches jewelry design and jewelry-making techniques locally and at bead shows around the country.

Connie Fox **jatayu.com**

Connie Fox, based in San Diego, California, has been making metal jewelry for more than a dozen years and has been teaching since 2001. Her classes focus on large-scale wirework, cold connections, metal fabrication, jewelry design, and enameling. She is an adjunct professor at San Diego Community College.

Kate Ferrant Richbourg **beaducation.com**

Kate Ferrant Richbourg of San Mateo, California, has been designing jewelry and teaching at national shows, bead societies, and bead shops since 1992 and is published in many jewelry magazines. She has appeared on *DIY Jewelry* and *Craft Lab,* and she currently rocks the director of education post at Beaducation.com.

Kriss Silva

Kriss Silva has been designing and teaching jewelry workshops since 1995. She views jewelry design as a creative outlet as well as a forum to share ideas. Kriss enjoys teaching as a way to express and foster her passion for the craft, evident in the metals, gemstones, and color combinations that she uses and in her bold aesthetics and unconventional approach to design. Kriss is based in Burlingame, California.

Tracy Stanley **wiredarts.net**

Tracy Stanley of Bellevue, Washington, loves the organic nature of wire and metal. Tracy has been an instructor for more than sixteen years and currently travels from coast to coast teaching wire and metal projects. Tracy is a partner in Wired Arts with Janice Berkebile.

Gallery Artists

Very special thanks to the fine jewelry artists who contributed to our gallery chapter:

Lisa Claxton lisaclaxton.blogspot.com
Lisa Dienst-Thomas lpjewelry.etsy.com
Lisa Leonard lisaleonardonline.com
Lori Ramotar artworkbylori.com
Randi Samuels studiodax.com

SOURCES FOR SUPPLIES

Look for local jewelry-making supply shops or try these online resources for everything you need to make the projects in this book.

Beaducation Inc. **beaducation.com**

Beaducation.com was founded by the author, Lisa Niven Kelly, to provide jewelry supplies and education to all. The site offers video classes, tools and materials for stamped metal jewelry and wirework, and design tips.

Rio Grande **riogrande.com**

Rio Grande is a comprehensive jewelry-making supply company.

Jatayu **jatayu.com**

Jatayu is the site and shop of jewelry artist Connie Fox, offering tools, supplies, and education.

Tandy Leather Factory **tandyleatherfactory.com**

Tandy Leather Factory offers leather products and supplies.

INDEX